FINANCIAL ABC's
of retirement planning

A simple-to-understand, non-Wall Street approach to conservative retirement planning

David P. Vick

A workbook based on the book "Bat-Socks, Vegas and Conservative Investing", by author David P. Vick
Second Edition

Copyright © 2012 David P. Vick.
All rights reserved.
ISBN 978-1-300-10762-0

This workbook was prepared to provide the reader with accurate and reliable information in regard to the subject matter covered. The advice and strategies contained herein may not be suitable for your situation. It is sold with the understanding that the publisher is not engaged in rendering legal, accounting, tax, or other professional services. If you require legal advice or the other expert services, you should pursue the help of a competent professional.

Financial ABC's of retirement planning

Workbook Topics

Section One: Introduction
- Disclosures   6
- Introduction   8
- Workshop Goals   10

Section Two: The Need for a New Model
1. **Bat-Socks, Vegas, & Conservative Investing   11**
   a. Conservative retirement planning?   11
   b. Upset-ness   12
   c. Risk vs. Reward   12
   d. Types of Risk   13
   e. Risk Tolerance Scale   13
   f. How to be Conservative When Planning for Retirement   14
   g. Benefits of Conservative retirement planning   14
2. **"What the heck just happened?"   17**
   a. Perspective & Paradigm Shifts   17
   b. Looking Back at the Dow from 1980   17
   c. Welcome to the M-Times   18
   d. Gambling vs. Investing   19
   e. Changes Out of Bear Markets   20
3. **Santa & Six Wall Street Myths   23**
   a. Myths or Maxims   23
   b. Wall Street Saying #1: I haven't Lost Until I Sell   23
   c. Wall Street Saying #2: Large Wire Houses   24
   d. Wall Street Saying #3: A diversified portfolio   25
   e. Wall Street Saying #4: Buy and Hold is an Effective Conservative Strategy   27
   f. Wall Street Saying #5: Just Buy an Index Fund   27
   g. Wall Street Saying #6: Index Annuities are Dangerous   28
4. **Jump in the Water's Fine!   31**
   a. A New Financial Planning Model. Really?   31
   b. The Status Quo Bias   31
   c. Wall Street is Disconnected with Main Street   32
   d. Ma & Pa LunchBucket & the Wall Street Model   34

Section Three: The ABC Planning Model

5. **Lego's, Train Sets, and the ABC Planning Model**   37
    a. Wall Street's Pyramids and Risk Tolerance   37
    b. A Conservative Planner's Dilemma   37
    c. The ABC Planning Model   38
    d. Category A: Cash   39
    e. Category B: Fixed Principal Assets   40
    f. Category C: Risk   42
    g. ABC Example   43
    h. Create Your Own ABC Model   44
    i. Types of Assets   45
    j. ABC Risk vs. Reward   45
    k. Rule of 100   46
    l. Major Differences Between Wall Street and the ABCs   47
6. **Who's the King?**   49
    a. The Goal of Yellow Money   49
    b. How Much Liquidity   50
    c. Yellow Money Categories   50
        i. Accessible with no penalties for withdrawal   50
        ii. Accessible with minimal penalties for withdrawal   51
    d. Savings, Not Investing   52
7. **"They are who we thought they were!"**   54
    a. Fixed Income Asset or Fixed Principal Asset?   54
    b. Three Green Money Rules   55
    c. What is an Annuity?   55
        i. Variable Annuities   56
        ii. Fixed & Fixed Indexed Annuities   57
        iii. Four Year FIA Graph   57
        iv. What are the Guarantees?   58
        v. How Does an FIA Credit Interest?   59
        vi. Any Fees in FIA's?   61
        vii. How About Liquidity?   62
    d. Laddered Maturities in FIA's   62
    e. Planning for Income with an FIA   64
    f. Guaranteed Withdrawal Benefits   65
8. **How's the Weather?**   69
    a. Red Money Planning   69
    b. Systematic Risk, Variance, and Volatility   69
    c. Beta, R-Squared, and Standard Deviation   70
    d. Stock-Type Risk & Bond-Type Risk   72
    e. Who Chooses the Assets?   73
    f. Tactical vs. Buy and Hold   73
9. **A Negative Neighbor**   77
    a. What if the worst Bear market in history happened again?   77
    b. Using the ABC Model in a Bear Market   78
    c. Why the ABC Model Works   80

Section Four: Retirement Planning Issues

10. The Cowboy Preacher   83
   a. Biggest Need for Retiree's: Income Planning   83
   b. Accumulation vs. Distribution   84
   c. Green Money Income Plans   86

11. I should have listened!   91
   a. 401(k) Plans: Remodel or Replace?   91
   b. Seven Problems With a 401(k)   91
       i. Problem #1: Is your 401(k) compliant?   91
       ii. Problem #2: Roth Accounts   92
       iii. Problem #3: Limited Choices   93
       iv. Problem #4: 20% Withholding Trap   94
       v. Problem #5: Limited Beneficiary Options   95
       vi. Problem #6: RMD Errors   98
       vii. Problem #7: The Non-Stretch Plan   98
   c. Understanding Your 401(k) Options   99

Section Five: Making Your Own ABC Plan

12. You Need a Sherpa!   102
   a. How to choose an advisor.   102
       i. Trust   102
       ii. Like-Ability   104
       iii. Competence   105
   b. Questions to Ask an Advisor   106
   c. Becoming a Client-Partner   107

13. Deal or No Deal   109
   a. Three Elements of a Financial Decision   109
       i. Logic   109
       ii. Beliefs   110
       iii. Emotions   112
   b. Process, Process, Process   113

14. Seven Steps to an ABC Plan   11
   a. Step 1: Get Your Assets Together   116
   b. Step 2: Write it Down   116
   c. Step 3: ABC Your Assets   117
   d. Step 4: Choose an Advisor   117
   e. Step 5: Process, Process, Process   118
   f. Step 6: Review & Adjust   118
   g. Step 7: Sleep Easy   118

Section Six: Appendixes

1. Asset Review Forms   121
2. Retirement Budget Forms   130
3. Risk Tolerance Questionnaire   132
4. Footnotes   135

FINANCIAL ABC's
of retirement planning

Disclosures

The information provided in these materials is for illustrative purposes only. Opinions, forecasts and recommendations are solely those of the author, including inflation rates and investment rates of return, are estimates only and in no way guarantee future performance. The assumptions and calculations are estimates and are meant to serve solely as a guideline. If any assumptions used in these materials are not realized, then the calculations will be inaccurate. There is no express or implied guaranty or warranty that any result shown will be achieved.

This information is not intended to give tax, legal, or investment advice. Please seek advice from a qualified professional on these matters. Annuity Contracts are products of the insurance industry and are not guaranteed by any bank or insured by the FDIC. When purchasing a fixed indexed annuity, you own an annuity contract backed by the insurance company, you are not purchasing shares of stocks or indexes. Product features such as interest rates, caps, and participation rates may vary by product and state and may be subject to change. Surrender charges may apply for early withdrawals. Be sure to review the specific product disclosure for more details. Guarantees are based on the financial strength and claims paying ability of the insurance company.

Lifetime income benefit riders are used to calculate lifetime payments only. The income account value is not available for cash surrender or in a death benefit. Excess withdrawals may reduce lifetime income and may incur surrender charges. Fees may apply. Guarantees based on the financial strength and claims paying ability of the insurance company. See specific product disclosure for more details.

Any statements or recommendations regarding annuities are solely those of the instructor teaching this course. Annuity guarantees are based on the claims-paying ability of the issuing insurance company. Annuity rates of return are based upon annuity contracts that are currently available in the marketplace. Actual rates of return will depend upon the specific terms of the annuity contract entered into between the client and insurance company. Rates of return on certain fixed indexed annuities may be calculated differently than the relevant market index and result in a lower return. Certain annuity features may require additional conditions and costs, and surrender charges for early withdrawals may result in a loss of principal. Withdrawals of earnings may be subject to ordinary income tax and, if taken prior to age 59 1/2, may be subject to a 10% federal tax penalty.

David P. Vick, Vick & Associates, Inc. makes no assertions on behalf of the financial advisor/instructor who uses this material in a workshop. In addition, the author has not in any way qualified the financial advisor/instructor that uses this material in a workshop, or conducted any background checks or government agency checks on them. We recommend that you interview the advisor thoroughly asking them for their background information, and check their references and listed credentials. Any advice you receive is the sole responsibility of the advisor giving the advice. David P. Vick, Vick & Associates, Inc., is not responsible for any financial advisor/instructor's action or failure to act in the best interest of the client. David P.

Vick, Vick & Associates, Inc., are not responsible for the advice or financial plans or any other services or investments or insurance products provided by the advisor/instructor. The use of the advisor/instructor who teaches this course is at your own risk. By using the advisor/instructor who teaches this course you are agreeing that David P. Vick, Vick & Associates, Inc. are in no way responsible or liable for any misconduct, negligence, of any type of any of the financial advisor/instructor who teaches this course. In using the advisor/instructor who teaches this course you agree to hold David P. Vick, Vick & Associates, Inc., harmless from any and all claims, liabilities, and losses resulting from or related to your use of the financial advisor/instructor who taught this course.

FINANCIAL ABC's
of retirement planning

Introduction

We want to sincerely thank you for your time and effort to participate in this workshop. Our hope is that you would, at the end of our time together, not only learn some ideas on how to accomplish your retirement goals, but also have had a good time doing it.

The ABC Planning Model was developed by David P. Vick, a financial planner, author, and speaker who trains financial planners across the country. Mr. Vick created the workshop for people age 50 and up who would like to have an alternate to the typical Wall Street approach to retirement planning. For most conservative people planning for retirement, Wall Street's approach usually involves more risk than people either know they have or want to have in their portfolios. We'll use much of Mr. Vick's material on conservative investing and apply it to retirement planning.

While this course covers many different topics and assets, one stands out as needing a little more attention for the conservative person financially: a Fixed Indexed Annuity. There has been much written in the media negatively concerning annuities. Recently, though, writers have seemed to come forward with a more educated and reasoned approach. This course makes no apologies for the use of annuities in financial planning, in fact answers the question *"Where do index annuities fit in a client's total portfolio of assets."* Since, financial planners from large to small firms nationwide are making a more prominent use of these products this course helps to define how those planning for retirement can make best use of them.

The financial planner who is teaching this course may or may not be licensed to sell securities. If they are not licensed, then according to the ABC Model their focus is in what we call the Green Money Column of fixed principal assets. They in essence are Green Money specialists, which is a term you will come to appreciate. This means they may educate you on some of the topics pertaining to securities; however they will not be advising you or evaluating your security portfolio. Rather, they will be helping you evaluate where the Green Money assets fit into your total portfolio. If however, they are securities licensed they will be able to help you in all phases of the ABC Planning Model.

The course is designed around the ABC Planning Concepts in Mr. Vick's book, "Bat-Socks, Vegas, and Conservative Investing" which you will receive as a resource for this course. The book covers some of the following topics:

- Who is a Conservative Retirement Planner?
- What is Conservative Planning?
- Risk Assessment
- Wall Street is Broken
- Six Wall Street Myths
- ABC Planning Model

- Three Green Money Rules
- Income Planning
- Laddered Maturities of Annuities
- Seven Problems with a 401k
- What if it Happened Again
- How to Find a Financial Planner
- Elements of a Financial Decision
- Seven Steps to an ABC Plan
- Developing a Retirement Budget

This workshop is designed in six sections which follow the chapters laid out in the book. At the end of our time together you will hopefully have made your very own retirement plan based on the ABC Model. This course is not a solicitation to sell any products or services. You paid a fee and have received the workbook, book, DVDs and hours of instruction from a professional. You may enjoy the training and hopefully it assists you in your pursuit of a conservative planning strategy.

However, though we know you have many options as far as financial planners are concerned and it is certainly not a requirement of this course, it is the instructor's hope that you would use their services to help you accomplish the success you desire in retirement planning.

Again, we appreciate your participation in this course of study and hope you enjoy it thoroughly.

Note: All materials from "Bat-Socks, Vegas and Conservative Investing, 2nd Edition" are in quotations and used by permission of David P. Vick.

FINANCIAL ABC's
of retirement planning

Workshop Goals

The Financial ABC's of Retirement Planning workshop seeks to help people age 50 and up develop a strategy for their retirement assets. We would like you to take a few minutes and jot down your initial thoughts regarding your expectations of this workshop and participate in the initial class discussion so your instructor can best mold the class to the needs of those present.

Name(s): _____

1. I was hoping this workshop would help me/us?

2. What is your current/former occupation?

3. What are your immediate concerns about your retirement assets?

4. What are your greatest concerns regarding your retirement goals?

5. Are you currently retired? ___ Yes ___No

   If not currently retired, do you plan on retiring? ___ Yes ___No
   If not currently retired, in how many years do you plan to retire? _____

6. When planning for retirement, how would you classify yourself?

   ___ Conservative
       ___ In-between Conservative and Moderate
   ___ Moderate
       ___ In-between Moderate and Aggressive
   ___ Aggressive

FINANCIAL ABC's
of retirement planning

Chapter One

Bat-Socks & Vegas
Conservative Retirement Planning

"Conservative investing is not like wearing Bat-socks. It's not a fad. It's not something you do for a few months and then try the next mutual fund flavor of the month. Conservative investing is core investing. Its long-haul investing.

There is a basic need for those who use this strategy, which is simply the need to sleep at night. They don't want to worry about losing money. They are not after quick market gains and fast money schemes."

1.1 **How would you describe a planning "fad?"**

1.2 **When the author talks about "conservative investing" not being a fad, what do you think he means?**

1.3 **How would you define conservative retirement planning?**

1.4 **What is "long haul" planning?"**

Upset-ness

"The investing community thinks in terms of "risk aversion" when it comes to assessing a person's "risk tolerance.""

When it comes to losing money, on a scale of 1-10 how "upset" do you get with fluctuations in the market? Put an X on the line below.

1 (I'm not upset at all)   (I'm jumping off a ledge) 10

"When you lose you get upset because you weren't in control. The degree of your "upset-ness" is the degree of your conservative nature."

1.5   **Have you ever been to Las Vegas? What has been your gambling experience?**

1.6   **Would you typically make a budget for gambling?**

1.7   **Do you get upset when you lose money gambling? Why or why not?**

"Wall Street, however, disconnects with Main Street by defining risk as "the chance that your actual return will be different than what you expected."(1) In other words, they define risk as the potential for your assets to gain *or* lose. Conservative investors laugh at the thought of gaining money as a risk. Instead a conservative investor defines risk as the potential to lose money. It's not a matter of return on your principal, but return of your principal. A conservative investor's aversion to risk, then, is how they feel about losing more than they expected."

Risk vs. Reward

"One of the fundamental ideas in finance is the concept of risk vs. reward. It is generally assumed that the greater the risk, the greater the potential return. For instance, a U.S. Treasury bond pays out less of a return than a corporate bond because the U.S. Government is less likely to go bankrupt than a corporation…the risk associated with the corporate bond pushes the issuer of that bond to offer a higher return."

Types of Risk

There are many types of risk. Here's a short list:
- Market risk
- Business risk
- Purchasing power risk (inflation)
- Sovereign risk
- Interest rate risk
- Reinvestment risk
- Liquidity risk
- Country risk
- Systematic risk
- Unsystematic risk
- Event risk
- Political risk
- Price risk

1.8　　Take the Risk Assessment Questionnaire located in Appendix 3.

Risk Tolerance Scale

Low　　　　　　　　Moderate　　　　　　　　Growth　　　　　　　　Aggressive
◆―――――――――――――――――――――――――――――――――◆

1.9　　What type of risk do you want when it comes to planning for your retirement? Put an X on the line which best describes your retirement planning choices. Explain your answer.

"Basically, how you feel about an adverse effect in your portfolio is your personal Risk Tolerance. For instance, let's say you experienced losses in 2000-2003 and again in 2008, but only to the degree at which the broad market suffered losses. You felt bad, yet you may have also believed your assets would recover over time, so you didn't lose any sleep over it. If that was true about you, you are at least a "moderate" on the scale.

On the other hand, imagine you are talking to a friend who had experienced the same losses as above. If you begin to get a pit in your stomach, your palms get all sweaty and you can't avoid the feeling of complete devastation even though it isn't even your money, you are definitely a "conservative" on the Risk Tolerance Scale. You are a conservative investor."

1.10　　From what you have read and discussed so far, would you describe yourself as conservative when planning for retirement? Why or why not?

How to be Conservative When Planning for Retirement: Life in the "Slow Lane"

"If risk avoidance is your heartbeat, then you have to realize patience is the key to conservative investing. Not patience in the sense of recovering from losses, but patience in accruing gains over a longer period of time. Lower risk assets typically are the tortoise, not the hare. While there have been times in history when fixed assets have had high yields, it isn't the norm."

1.11   What are the highest interest rates you remember receiving on bank assets?

"High interest rates seem to cycle through history over longer periods of time. If you are waiting for high interest rates, you are going to have a nice relaxing wait. The truth is that 6-month CD rates from 2000 through 2009 have had a high around 7% and a low of something under 1%. (2)

People using an interest rate strategy make good use of bank deposits, money markets, U.S. Treasuries, and fixed-income assets. For the most part, these assets provide relative security of principal, yet lower returns. The real problem is the loss of purchasing power due to high inflation, which often accompanies times of elevated interest rates."

If you are conservative in your approach to retirement planning there seems to be a rather small amount of financial options. In a later chapter we will discuss some of the "fixed principal options" you might use in your portfolio.

Benefits of Conservative Retirement Planning: Who would want to go through this?

"The major league benefit to the ultra-conservative investor who doesn't risk principal is simple: sleep. That's right. They don't worry about their assets when the DOW drops 300 points in a day. They wonder how that poor sucker with his money in the market is doing, and silently gloat."

1.12   Have you ever "silently gloated" about the safety of your assets? Explain.

1.13   Would you like to "silently gloat" about the safety of your assets? Explain.

1.14 **What is conservative retirement planning and how would you implement such a strategy? Explain.**

"Simply put, conservative investing is a long-term strategy to manage risk in such a way as to conserve principal while maintaining buying power. What are lower-risk assets? Well, they could be anything.

The real question is, "how do you manage risk?"

1.15 **What do you think the author means when he says, "The real question is how you manage risk?**

Chapter One Notes

FINANCIAL ABC's
of retirement planning

Chapter Two

What the Heck Just Happened?
Retirement Planning Paradigm Shifts

When we look over the last 30 to 40 years in the financial planning community, there seems to be large paradigm shifts in the American culture that have affected the way they plan for retirement. Recognizing these changes in the way our culture views their retirement savings can be a key to successful retirement.

"What is a paradigm shift? You can think of it as a sort of transformation, a changing of one way of thinking to another. Some might even call it a revolution or a metamorphosis."

2.1 How would you think paradigm shifts in culture and history affect retirement planning?

"There are also very interesting alterations in "investing paradigms" which have taken place over the last 30 to 40 years. Changes of this magnitude usually take a long time to blossom. I believe our perspective on investing has changed because of a cultural transformation in America and the effect of bear markets—especially big bear markets—on future economies."

Looking Back at the Dow from 1980

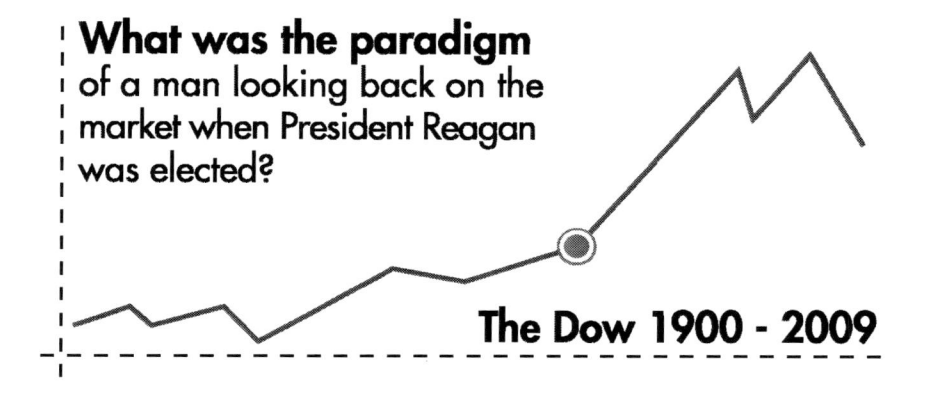

What was the paradigm of a man looking back on the market when President Reagan was elected?

The Dow 1900 - 2009

"If you were an investor in 1980, when President Ronald Reagan was elected, what did you see? I mean, if you could literally stand on a time line of the DOW in 1980 and peer backward over the last ten to twenty years, what would you see that would affect how you invested going forward? The 70's were turbulent financial years with investors largely investing in bonds, large cap mutual funds, and blue chip stocks. The 70's were the up and down years of a mid-term bear market that started in the fall of 1965 and didn't recover until the fall of 1982, covering 17 restless years. Who can forget long gas lines and double-digit inflation? That's what you saw looking back from 1980.

The prevalent investor strategy at the beginning of the 80's was unmistakably conservative. They looked for safety and dividends. They weren't "speculative" in nature, but desired small, consistent gains along with dividends. Not much risk."

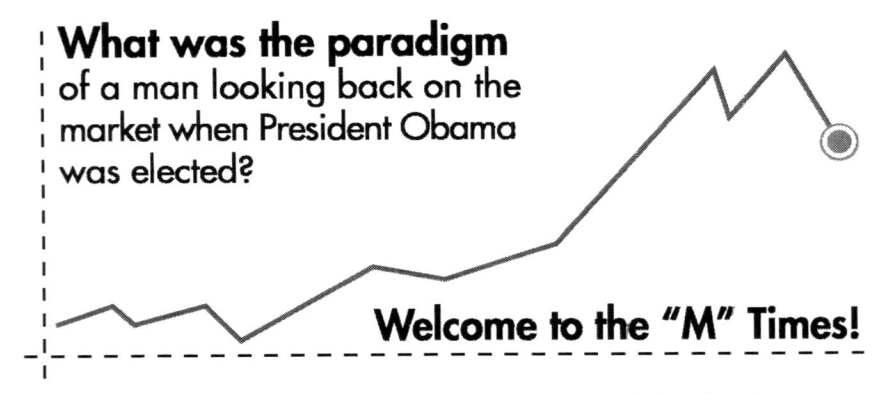

What was the paradigm of a man looking back on the market when President Obama was elected?

Welcome to the "M" Times!

"In contrast, what was the view of an investor looking back on the market when President Obama took office in 2009? Again, if you could stand on a DOW timeline and look back, what would you see?

An investor looking back on the last 20 years in the DOW would see a huge M in the graph the closer it got to his time—the "irrational exuberance" of the 1990's Bull market, followed by a tech bubble bursting into a near 50% loss from 2000-2002, followed by a 5-year Dow run up with the peak of the second half of the "M" in October of 2007, followed by the housing bubble, bank bubble, finance bubble, and whatever other bubble was out there, bursting into flames by the low point of March 2009."

2.2 **What is your reaction to the high volatility of the M-times, especially when you think of planning for your retirement?**

"First, some are numb from the terrifying roller coaster rides and leave their money in the market not knowing what to do but hoping it will come back. It's called Buy and Hope, which we'll discuss later. Second, others are cashing out and are investing in low-interest-rate CD's, money markets, and savings accounts. There is a ton of money on the sidelines. Mass confusion reigns."

Gambling vs. Investing: A New Paradigm Shift

2.3 What was the American perception of gambling in the 1950's and 1960's? Was it positive or negative?

"In·vest" verb
1. *to commit (money) in order to earn a financial return.(2)*

2.4 What does the dictionary's definition of invest imply to you?

"gam·ble" verb
1. *a: to play a game for money or property b: to bet on an uncertain outcome*
2. *to stake something on a contingency: take a chance* (3)

2.5 Which definition above is more in line with our current financial planning culture? Why?

In his book titled *Blind Faith*, published in 2003 Ed Winslow makes an interesting case for the cultural changes brought on by the cultural acceptance of gambling over the last thirty years. Take a look at the facts on Gambling:

- Gambling is a $90 billion a year industry.
- 1988— only legal in Nevada and New Jersey.
- 1994 – Operating in 23 states.
- 2000 – Over 34 million people visited Las Vegas.
- 2000 – Over 127 million in casinos nationally.
- 2003 – Operating in 48 states
- Industry take - $750 per participant or $250 per person in U.S. (5)

"If you've been to Vegas in the last 10 years, you surely can't miss the fact it is a retiree's haven. The very people who, when they were growing up, thought of gambling as evil, have now made Risk City their number one travel destination. Not only that, but some of the most popular cable TV shows are televised gambling events. You can watch it on television and play it online 24 hours a day. It is in our 21st century

American blood. The acceptance of gambling represents a definite cultural shift and has doubtlessly had an effect on not only the way we invest, but if we invest at all!"

2.6 **In what ways would the average person's perspective change with a large cultural shift toward the acceptance of gambling?**

2.7 **What changes would the conservative planner make in their portfolio when influenced by a gambling culture?**

"Strangely enough, in 1978 Congress enacted a change in the tax code which enabled much of the change to speculation in our investing culture. They amended Section 401(k). It took effect in 1980, and by 1983 more than half of large companies were setting up 401k plans, a little more than 17,000.(6) Half way through the 1980's, there were less than 8 million people investing in 401ks with about $100 billion invested. By 2006, there were seventy million participants and more than $3 trillion invested.(7) The average American in the 70's wasn't invested in the market, and by 2006 it's a cultural norm. They went from saving in banks to investing in mutual funds just because of the availability? No. There has to be a correlation between our society's acceptance of gambling and the radical flight from safety to speculation. Again, what the heck just happened?"

2.8 **How has the availability of 401(k) plans impacted the way the average American plans for retirement?**

Changes Coming Out of Bear Markets

"In 1884 Charles Dow began publishing his "Dow Jones Averages" in the *Customer's Afternoon Letter,* which was the forerunner of *The Wall Street Journal.* In 1896, he changed the name to the *Dow Jones Industrial Average,* which consisted of twelve industrial stocks, a departure from the original nine railroad stocks, and two industrial stocks. The first index containing the "Rails," as people referred to it, continued to rival the industrial average's for the next 20 years.(8)

Russell Napier, in his book *The Anatomy of a Bear* tells us these two main indexes, the Dow Jones Industrials and the "Rails" Stock index, were the two main indexes at the turn of the 1900's. During the hard financial times from 1900-1914 and the start of World War I, Napier tells us that the government nationalized the railroads, and guess what happened to that stock index. Right, it virtually went away when the government devalued the rail stocks by their takeover.(9) That was a huge alteration in the market.

Another event that caused a deviation in the market was the creation of the Federal Reserve in 1914. The Fed was created to make our currency "elastic."(10) In other words, to "inflate" the money supply during a recession or depression, the fed would print more money tied very loosely to the gold standard hoping it would grow the economy. That created incredible changes in the financial markets coming out of 1921."

2.9 What similarities are there to the government involvement during the first 20 years of the twentieth century and the last 10 years?

2.10 How might this affect the economy and the stock market?

2.11 If you are unsure of the changes that will come out of a large Bear market, how would you plan differently?

You should have a solid plan to manage risk that matches your conservative risk tolerance. Remember, the question is not how much money you should have in a mutual fund or even the fund's 3, 5, and 10 year returns, but how you manage risk. That's the question!

Chapter Two Notes

FINANCIAL ABC's
of retirement planning

Chapter Three

Santa & Six Wall Street Myths
Financial Planning Myths

Myths or Maxims?

"One way Webster's dictionary defines myth is by describing it as a popular belief that has come about by "an unfounded or false notion." Maxim on the other hand, is defined by Webster's as a general truth, or a fundamental principle."

Wall Street Saying #1: "I haven't lost until I sell"

3.1 In the past, when your statement showed a loss did you tell yourself that you hadn't really lost anything yet?

"This Wall Street saying actually comes from a reality in the world of taxes. If you bought a stock for $10 a share, and four years later it's worth $20 a share, you have good news. You made money. If you sell the asset at this point, you will have a gain to report on your taxes of $10 a share. You have "realized" your gain. You also have some bad news, a tax due on the gain. This is called a "capital gains tax," which is a tax on the gain in the asset. You are only taxed if you sell the asset, thus you "realize" the gain only by selling the asset.

If however, the share price went down to $5 a share, you have lost money in your investment, and if you sell, you will "realize" a loss. You can use that loss on your tax return to wipe out certain gains. You would not be able to use this to your advantage on your tax returns, unless you sold. In reality, you haven't lost until you sell, is only true when it comes to taxes. It is not true when it comes to investing."

3.2 Do you sometimes suspect a broker's motives? If so, in what ways?

"People will often want to believe a lie because the truth is too painful to live with. They are in total disbelief of the realities communicated in their statement. The same broker, however, will call them when their assets have grown in value bragging, "See how much money I've made you? Don't you want to invest more?"

"If "I haven't lost until I sold" is true, then all bad mortgages would just be a paper loss and the black abyss of 2008 would never have happened. The mindset that an actual loss of value in any asset is only a "paper loss" is the way creative accounting starts. There are no paper losses when it comes to investing. There is only lost money. Sure, you can write it off your taxes, but that is my point exactly. It's a tax reality. For investors, we can't afford to be unrealistic in our outlook, especially in our beliefs about money. We can't afford to take a soft passing glance at our statements and believe a convenient lie."

3.3   **Do you believe that when it comes to money "you have what you have?" Explain.**

"The truth is the market goes up and down. Your accounts may very well recover to their old levels, but until then, "you have what you have" is a better catch phrase to use. Reality is always a better place to begin when evaluating how to move forward. You can even say that you have lost money in your investments and if you keep them they may one day regain their value. I'm sure that's what the owners of Enron stock said."

3.4   *I haven't lost until I sell.* **Is it a Myth or Maxim?**

Wall Street Saying #2: "The large wire houses are the best place to get professional advice."

> *A long time ago, a visitor from out of town came to a tour in Manhattan. At the end of the tour, they took him to the financial district. When they arrived to Battery Park, the guide showed him some nice yachts anchoring there, and said, "Here are the yachts of our bankers and stockbrokers."*
>
> *"And where are the yachts of the investors?" asked the naive visitor. (1)*

"In case you are unsure what a "wire house" is, it is a large brokerage firm with many branch offices and brokers. The branch offices operate under the jurisdiction of the main firm, share financial information and research through a common computer system. Past large wire-house firms which you might be familiar with are Merrill Lynch, Morgan Stanley, Goldman Sachs, Wells Fargo, or Wachovia. Since 2008, it has gotten a little hard to keep up with these firms because of the meltdowns and mergers."

3.5   **Why do you believe people planning for retirement would be attracted to large wire house firms?**

"...After 2008 and 2009, brokers began to consider the possibility that large wire house firms might be more of a liability than a benefit to their careers. The independent advisor used to be looked on as a second-class option for those seeking financial advice. However, many brokers who are leaving the failed large wire houses are going independent. (2) Clearly, they see the need to disassociate themselves with the Wall Street muck being exposed in the daily news.

In typical Wall Street fashion, these firms were selling stocks, proprietary mutual funds and IPOs to their clients who believed they were receiving unbiased advice. The reality is, they were being sold products which best suited the firm's bottom line rather than bettering the client's positions. Their fiduciary responsibility was in question, and the public began to realize it. Lawsuit after lawsuit began to show a broken culture's motivations were highly suspect.

In addition, if you only go to the large wire houses for advice, then you leave out the largest group of advisors who happen to be independent. Most of these advisors are highly qualified professionals with the client's best interests at heart. They don't want any part of a large company telling them what they have to "sell" their clients. They are independent insurance agents, Registered Investment Advisors, and brokers with smaller independent firms concentrating on the needs of individuals as a priority."

3.6 *Large wire houses are the best place to get professional advice.* **Is it a Myth or Maxim?**

Wall Street Saying #3: "A diversified portfolio of stocks, bonds, and mutual funds are safe over the long haul."

"Wide diversification is only required when investors do not understand what they are doing."
Warren Buffett (3)

3.7 **If you didn't have a clue about the market, how wise is it to place a major portion of your assets in the market?**

3.8 **Does diversification actually provide the safety a conservative planner desires?**

"…Basically, diversification implies you can reduce your overall risk by investing in assets which move in different directions over time and in response to market conditions. You might buy individual stocks and bonds, large cap and small cap, domestic and foreign, financial sector and manufacturing sectors, hoping that if one asset class goes south the other area will go north. This has been the practice for Wall Street firms for decades, based on years of studies.

In an editorial for Investment Advisor Magazine, July 2009 an advisor, commenting on the market collapse in 2008 and 2009, makes the point that Wall Street was broken (again!) and the diversification models used by wealth management advisors failed their largest test ever. The author suggests the following reason:

> *"What went wrong? The fixed income substitutes pushed by the major investment houses" low volatility hedge funds, preferred stocks, asset-backed securities or other structured products, closed-end bond funds, income/mortgage REITs, and master limited partnerships weren't fixed income substitutes at all. None of them is a substitute for the most important characteristic that investors should be looking for from the fixed income portion of their portfolios: safety of principal." (4)*

3.9 **What assets do you believe could be listed on the fixed income portion of a statement?**

"The editorial goes on to imply that bonds are the only fixed-income asset that should be used to balance risk in portfolios for investors seeking a safe diversification. The problem with bonds, which we'll discuss in a later chapter, is they can also lose money. If you held Bear Stearns bonds, or Lehman Brothers bonds, or if you currently hold California municipal bonds, you may very well have experienced losses or soon will. At the very least, you are or were very nervous."

3.10 **As a conservative person planning for retirement, what lessons could you learn from the severe market losses in a year like 2008?**

3.11 *A diversified portfolio of stocks, bonds, and mutual funds are safe over the long haul.* **Is it a Myth or Maxim?**

Wall Street Saying #4: *"Buy & Hold* is an effective conservative strategy"

*"Buy and hold as a strategy is very questionable…
It's worked in the past, but in time of severe market stress it just doesn't work."*
Ben Stein, author, lawyer, actor, and financial commentator (5)

"The simple reason "buy & hold" is better named "buy & hope" is because it lacks the ability to respond to markets in a timely manner. I will be covering much of this in chapter 8, but tactical management, in my opinion, is a more up-to-date management style for conservative investors. The average broker or investment advisor does the best he can by picking stocks, bonds and mutual funds that fit a client's risk tolerance. Then for the most part, they sit on those assets come hell or high water, only liquidating in extreme situations. The reasons they change assets are to try to find "relative strength" in a sector or under-priced assets in a growing segment of the economy. Some use outside sources to get counsel on where they should invest next. These sources are investment advisors themselves trying to figure out the market. Usually what happens is the advisor picks a hot mutual fund manager and hopes he continues his track record. The whole system seems to look at returns over 1 year, 3 years, and 5 years to see who has the best record, or which fund or stock is "on the rise."

The problem with this mentality is it doesn't have a solid plan for how to manage risk. The markets do two things very well: they go up and they go down. Volatility is inherent in the markets. How you deal with volatility and risk should be the focus, not trying to compare returns. Comparing returns is tempting and you can make a case that certain fund managers have done well over time. Yet, everybody lost in 2008. When fear and panic set in, a buy and hold strategy will kill a retiree's portfolio. A fund manager has to pick stocks and in an environment like 2008 where the normal logic went out of the market, the fund manager was lost. He certainly couldn't sell everything, that's just not how they do it. And so they sat and painfully watched as their mutual funds value plummeted."

3.12 ***"Buy and Hold" is an effective conservative strategy.* Is it a Maxim or Myth?**

Wall Street saying #5: "Just buy a no-load index fund."

"Let's say you were a conservative-minded investor in 2000 that didn't buy into the tech-bubble and invested heavily in the S&P 500 Index. You listened to John Bogle, founder of Vanguard, and purchased no-load, low expense index funds from several sources, investing $500,000. You were 55 years old and looking to retire in January 1, 2010, at age 65. Here is what happened to you."

	S&P 500 from 2000-2009(6)	
	S&P 500	**Your Account**
January 3, 2000	1455.22	$500,000
December 31, 2009	1115.10	$383,150
	-23.37% Loss	

"Obviously, this is an over simplified illustration and you probably didn't have all of your money invested in the index funds. However, if you listened to the advice of those who believed this was a conservative strategy, you would have been incredibly disappointed with the funds you allotted to this strategy. Even if one third of your retirement accounts were in fixed assets that averaged 3%, over the decade you still would have lost about 8%."

3.13 **The important question is, could you retire with those types of losses or would you feel you might have to continue working?**

3.14 **Would you be willing to gamble your retirement on the above illustration not happening again?**

3.15 *Just buy an Index Fund.* **Is it a Maxim or Myth?**

Wall Street Saying #6: "Index annuities are dangerous"

"There are tons of articles railing on Fixed Index Annuities (FIA), by supposed experts quoting their own research. Yet none of them compare with the most recent study completed in 2008 by David F. Babbel, Professor of Insurance and Finance, at the University of Pennsylvania's, Wharton School of Business.

Tom Cochrane interviewed Professor Babbel for AnnuityDigest.com. He is quoted in Mr. Cochrane's blog, July 2009:

> "There has been a lot of misinformation in the popular press regarding FIAs. The vast majority of newspaper and magazine accounts vilify FIAs based on the results of alleged academic studies. The in-depth studies we conducted took over two years to complete and involved six Ph.D. financial economists and a pair of very well-known senior actuaries....Our findings regarding actual products show that since their inception in 1995 they have performed quite well – in fact, some have performed better than many alternative investment classes (corporate and government bonds, equity funds, money markets) in any combination." (7)

Professor Babbel's study actually shows when FIAs are compared to alternatives like Vanguard's S&P 500 Index Fund, money markets, and the S&P 500 itself, gave better returns since 1995, and for each year they were issued. He makes the case that for those investors who have a conservative to moderate risk tolerance, FIAs provide what these investors desire."

3.16 Do you believe a rational person would choose an Indexed Annuity? Why or Why not?

"Contrary to what some critics have stated, Babbel asserts that "Moderately risk-averse individuals will always choose the annuity over alternative investments." While the critics of FIAs have questioned whether people who could invest in alternative investments such as Treasury securities and equity mutual funds would not rationally invest in FIAs. Babbel concludes that many rational investors would actually prefer annuities over alternative investments. (8)"

3.17 *Index annuities are dangerous.* **Is it a Maxim or Myth?**

A comment about independent brokers who are a vital part of the financial planning community:

"In fact, the independent brokers who are out of the large wire house system are a hard-working crew with the best of intentions and, more often than not, excellent abilities. They are often well-trained and well-educated professionals. It's the myths that the culture perpetuates and the bias it comes from that need to change."

Financial ABC's of retirement planning

Chapter Three Notes

FINANCIAL ABC's
of retirement planning

Chapter Four

Jump in the Waters Fine
The Need for a New Planning Model

A new financial planning model? Really? Feel like jumping in?

"Whenever someone starts to talk about change, people get just a little nervous, kind of like leaping into an ice-cold lake. They are especially anxious when it involves their finances. As I bring up the subject of a "new model of investing," people are stopped cold at the end of the dock, not wanting to jump in. The status quo looks so good because it's the "known vs. the unknown," the warm and worn, yet rickety dock versus the potentially cold waters of a new investment model."

The Status Quo Bias

"Financial researchers tell us it's the "status quo bias" keeping us from jumping into a new model, even though the new model may be a better one:

> *"Most real decisions, unlike those of economics texts, have a status quo alternative—that is, doing nothing or maintaining one's current or previous decision. A series of decision-making experiments shows that individuals disproportionately stick with the status quo. Data on the selections of health plans and retirement programs…reveal that the status quo bias is substantial in important real decisions." (1)*

When faced with a decision between the dock and the water, we tend to stay on the dock, rather than risk plunging into a new environment."

4.1 **Have you ever been afraid of doing something a financial planner might have recommended?**

4.2 **Is it possible that staying with the same plan you have had for years, without making adjustments, might create adverse results for your retirement? If so, how?**

Wall Street is Disconnected from Main Street

"…the conservative investor is confused by Wall Street. Huge dollars, mega-deals, hot cars, expensive suits, fancy jewelry, and greedy advisors who each week it seems pull off investment scams bilking average investors out of their retirement savings. It seems like there is just no conscience. The government regulators seem inadequate and unable to stop the onslaught of Wall Street greed.

What is the typical Wall Street model of investing? To begin with, it is based on a "greed is good" philosophy. Once you understand who it's "good" for, you will know why people get so discouraged."

4.3 **Is greed good? Explain.**

4.4 **What affect does the disconnected "greed is good" philosophy of Wall Street have on the average American planning for retirement, if any?**

"Typically, Ma & Pa Lunchbucket are conservative investors who would like a plan designed specifically around their risk tolerance. What they actually receive is a diversified portfolio of market assets and asset classes managed in a "buy and hold" strategy with little movement over the years. Ma & Pa's "unique" portfolio consists of a basket of proprietary mutual funds, a variable annuity and possibly some blue chip stock, maybe even a bond or two. The mutual funds will be C-shares, which allow the broker to make a 1% trailer commission on Ma & Pa's assets with no motivation to change them over the years. They may receive one or two B-share funds, which carry penalties if you sell out of them too early, so you will be discouraged from leaving his services."

4.5 **Do fees affect your decisions about which assets you would choose? Explain.**

> **What are A, B, & C mutual fund shares?**
>
> Mutual fund share classes are a way for the broker to receive commissions and the mutual fund company to structure expenses.
>
> - **A-Shares** have an up-front load which is deducted from your initial investment and a small trailer commission called a 12b1 fee. A–shares usually have lower expenses.
>
> - **B-Shares** have a back-end charge for early redemption and a trailer commission called a 12b1 fee. If you redeem your fund in a certain period of time, usually 5 to 8 years, you have a deferred sales charge. B-shares usually have higher expenses, but convert to A-shares at a certain point in time, thus reducing their expenses.
>
> - **C-Shares** usually have a 1% ongoing load every year. Commonly they have a small back-end charge that disappears after a year, lower expenses than B-shares, but higher expenses than A-shares. Typically good for short term investors.

"The second problem with Wall Street is it is too complicated. Wall Street forces you to rely on the professional to not just acquire the investments needed, but to decide *for* you what conservative looks like in a plan. The professional broker is swimming in the water saying, "Jump in!" Understandably, most conservative investors do not have a clue when it comes to evaluating and choosing stocks, bonds, mutual funds, annuities, or even know what a REIT is. They don't even know the majority of money markets are not FDIC insured! They are standing at the edge of the investing dock, anxiously wondering if this chattering teethed broker in the water knows what he's talking about with no way of being sure."

4.6 **Which financial commentators or shows do you listen to or watch? How much do you rely on financial commentators for your retirement planning information?**

4.7 **Put an X on the line below which represents how much you rely on financial commentators for your financial information. Explain your answer.**

Not at all   Not much   A little bit   Somewhat   A lot   Listen Daily

"Financial commentators in the media are looked upon as the investment guru for millions. It's not that these media moguls are bad people or that they even give poor advice. They simply do not know who you are or your specific needs. They also assume you, the average conservative investor, know what the heck they're talking about when they recommend "no-load, sector funds..."or any other asset. Even if you did figure out what they were talking about, they didn't tell you where it fit in your portfolio of assets.

Remember, a media personality's number one job is to sell "air-time" and their next book. Their job description does not include finding out your specific situation and emotional response to market losses, make a plan that fits your needs and then review that plan on a regular basis."

Ma & Pa Lunchbucket & the Wall Street Model

"Here's what the average experience is for Ma & Pa Lunchbucket trying to follow the Wall Street Model of Investing. They go to a seminar sponsored by a major brokerage firm's local office, conducted by a professional who is probably getting money for the cost of the workshop from some investment company who wants to promote their products. They sign a "complimentary consultation" form and head in for a visit with a supposedly "unbiased, trusted" advisor.

Mr. & Mrs. LB enter the offices and are shown the conference room. The broker is impressively dressed and surrounded by the aura of a Wall Street firm. Ma & Pa unveil their assets to the broker's waiting hand who says, "Not to worry...we'll take good care of you." The two conservative investors take a "risk-tolerance" exam to determine their feelings about gains and losses in a portfolio. They talk about goals and time lines, kids and grandkids, realities and dreams. Mr. LB tells of the last broker they were with and how they got burned and how they want safety with as little risk as possible. The broker acknowledges their concerns, telling them about the history of the prestigious firm for which he works. Mrs. LB is nodding approvingly. The broker invites them back in a week to hear the details of his specialized plan made specifically for Mr. & Mrs. LB. They leave with hope that the water may indeed be fine, this time.

Mr. & Mrs. LB come back for a plan they believe is designed just for them. Instead, they receive a cookie cutter group of investments the broker has been trained to sell. After viewing so many client statements from wire houses, I can actually predict what assets will be on the statement based on the company doing the investing. It is common knowledge among industry professionals that each major firm has a very predictable recommendation for each client. It may vary only by degree, but brokers are encouraged to make sales of the companies who own proprietary mutual funds and other assets that profit the investment firm *over other, better, and more appropriate assets.*"

4.8 **Have you ever had an experience like Ma & Pa LunchBucket? Explain.**

"The final reason Ma & Pa LunchBucket need a new model is that Wall Street wire houses themselves don't believe in their own system.

> *"After a decade of pushing fee-based services, Wall Street is slashing and burning the infrastructure that has supported the business. The moves threaten to damage the long-term health of the wirehouse business model for financial advisers and their clients.*
>
> *On the new Wall Street, wire houses are gutting the home office staff that has driven the growth of fee-based business...Even getting a simple phone call returned from the home office is turning into a trial. Forget about one-on-one attention."* (2)

Remember, Wall Street has long run on the motto, "greed is good." This philosophy places those who sell the assets at the top of the food chain and the clients who buy the assets just plain camel fodder. So, if you feel like Wall Street's disconnected voice is calling to you saying, "come on in, the water's fine," get off the dock as soon as possible!"

4.9 Do you believe the financial services community could use a new model to help consumers develop their financial plan? Explain.

Financial ABC's of retirement planning

Chapter Four Notes

FINANCIAL ABC's
of retirement planning

Chapter Five

Lego's, Train Sets, & the ABC Planning Model
The ABC Planning Model Defined

Wall Street's Pyramids and Risk Tolerance

"Wall Street's typical model of investing starts with the "Pyramid of Assets" and moves on to "Asset Allocation" models, which seem anything but easy or simple to understand... , these models depend on the broker knowing your "risk tolerance," which is the degree of uneasiness an investor is willing to experience when there is volatility in their portfolio."

A Conservative Planner's Dilemma

"Take Silvio and Lenora for instance. They are one of my all-time favorite client-partners. Lenora has told me more than once how she can't get to sleep at night. She's a worrier and a night owl. She doesn't think she would be able to sleep at all if they had money in the market. They don't want any market risk whatsoever. They understand the market goes up and it goes down and want to know only two things about their investments.

First, is their money safe from market losses, and second, are they beating CD's? They want that "in between space" of bank-type savings and market risk assets.

Silvio and Lenora are the type of investors who loves the ABC Model of Investing. They intuitively want the majority of their assets not open to market losses. Unlike Silvio and Lenora, some conservative investors will have a small to moderate percentage of their assets in the market. The problem is there are not many choices for this type of an investor. They struggle for years with low interest rates and long for the good old days of 12-15% CD's!"

A few questions:

5.1 Do you the conservative planner; know how to allocate your money to avoid the volatility which costs you sleepless nights?

5.2 How do you currently determine which assets to use and why you might use them?

5.3 Can an average person really understand why his or her money is placed in one asset over another? Explain.

5.4 Do you ever wonder if you need a degree in finance to understand how to allocate your assets? Explain.

5.5 Have you found a simple way to understand how to allocate your assets to accomplish your goals? Explain.

The ABC Model Planning Model

"First, imagine all your investible assets are liquid and we could arrange them in any way you like. That includes all your CD's, money markets, annuities, stocks, bonds, mutual funds, REITs, or whatever. It would be everything except your real estate, all liquid with no strings attached. Next, let's make a plan starting today.

You will have to imagine your assets not where they are invested today, or last year, or even where they were 10 years ago. We're not looking in the rear-view mirror, but trying to map out our future. This is vitally important, because you want to have your investments set up for your needs going forward, not left in accounts that might jeopardize your future. Of course, I realize not all of your assets are actually liquid and in a position to move to your ideal situation. This exercise will give you a glimpse of what you value in the types of assets in which you might invest and how to allocate them."

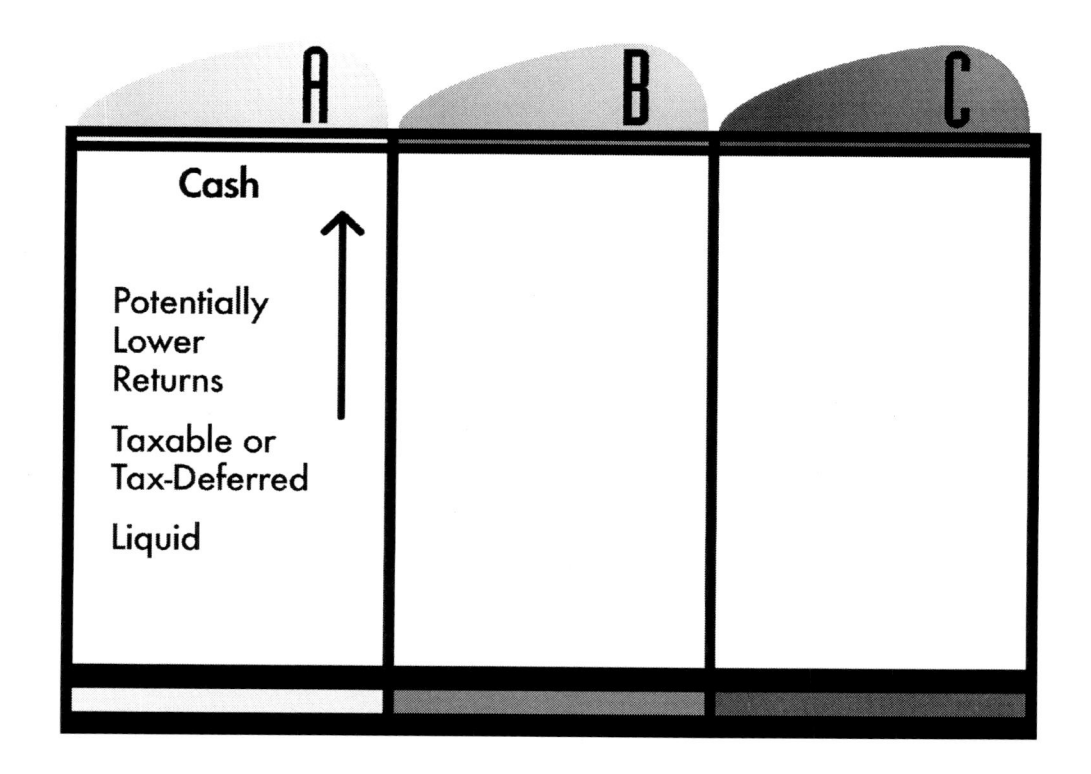

Category A: Cash

"Let's divide assets into categories, A, B, and C, which represent three types of assets. Category A is your cash reserves. Cash assets potentially carry low returns, but the principal is guaranteed and interest is compounded. According to the Federal Reserve, the average 6-month CD rate from 1990-2009 was 4.37% (20 years); 2000-2009 was 3.32% (10 years); from 2005-2009 it was 3.99% (5 years).(1) It is interesting to note the average inflation rate from 2000-2009 was 2.57%, which leaves the five year return averaging less than 1.5% before taxes. (2)

These accounts are typically taxable and have optimum liquidity. However, they can also be set up in various tax advantaged strategies such traditional IRA's, Roth IRA's, etc. Most often, these are bank-held assets like CD's, savings accounts, and money markets.

Financial advisors will often refer to this as short-term money, or emergency funds. If your furnace breaks down, your roof leaks, or you have a medical emergency, category A is where you save for such an occurrence. If you are saving for an exciting vacation or a new car, this is where the money goes. It is also where you might want to keep a savings account to replace any income lost due to a prolonged illness, injury, or job loss. Commonly, financial advisors will tell you to have six months to a year of income put away for these instances. The illustration below shows Column A assets. Imagine them as "Yellow Money" accounts."

A | **B** | **C**

Cash

Potentially Lower Returns

Taxable or Tax-Deferred

Liquid

Protected Growth

Potentially Moderate Returns

Tax-Deferred

Offer Partial Withdrawals

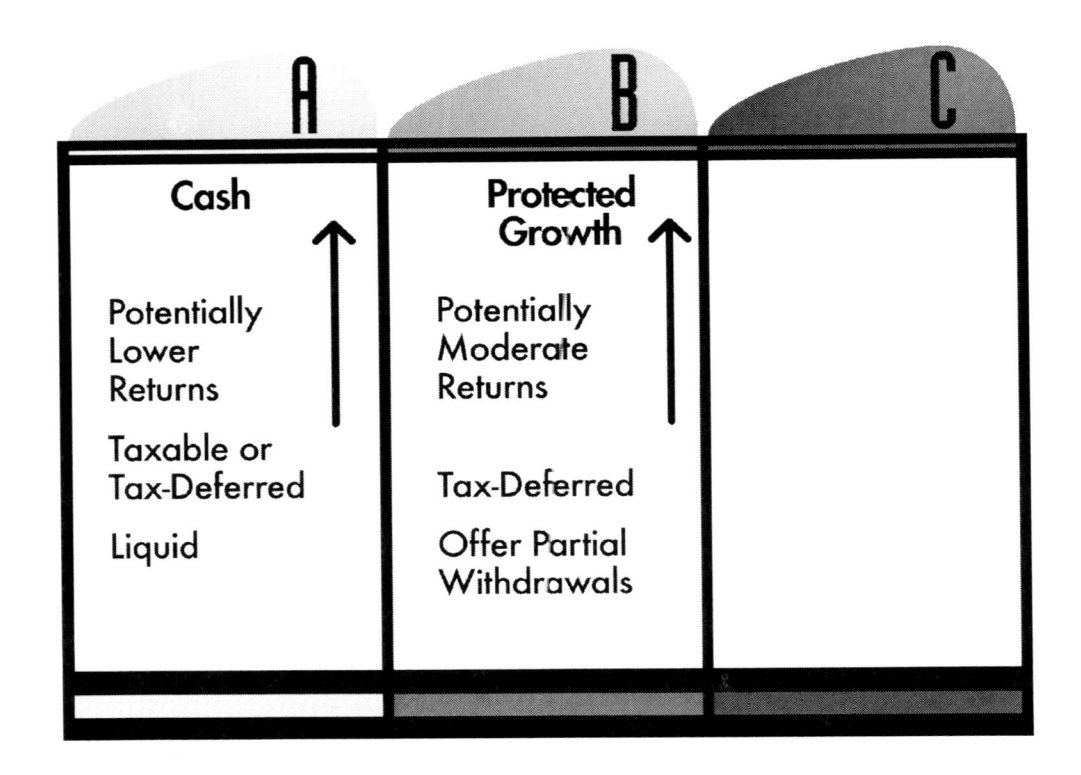

Category B: Fixed Principal Assets

"The second category is Column B, the "Green Money" column, and holds Protected Growth assets. They offer potentially moderate returns, are tax-deferred and offer partial withdrawals. The principal is protected, and previous years' gains are retained as interest. The annual returns on these assets vary greatly. In my own practice I have seen them yield from 0% to as high as 16%. Some include bonuses from 3% to 8%. These assets are designed to be the middle ground between CD's and the market. During the five-year period from October of 2004 through September of 2008, Index annuities averaged 5.42%, while CD's averaged 2.78%. (3)

I prefer using fixed indexed annuities in column B, which link the interest credits to the performance of a market index, such as the S&P 500, S&P Midcap 400, DOW, Russell 2000, Euro Dow, etc. Column B money is set aside for a longer period, often 5-10 years. Annuities have strings attached for withdrawals, but can be an excellent source of income over a lifetime. In other words, don't allocate money to the B column in which you would need more than 10% of next year, especially considering there could be a tax penalty on certain withdrawals prior to age 59 ½.

Generally assets in this column offer only partial withdrawals without a penalty, yet many include riders that waive surrender fees in the event of a nursing home stay or terminal illness. Indexed annuities are designed to function as the middle ground between lower interest rates of bank and savings accounts, and potential higher returns of risk oriented market money.

This is the Fixed Principal Asset column, where the principal is protected. The ABC Model looks at Fixed Income Assets different than Wall Street does. Over the years, Wall Street has used a laddered portfolio of bonds to accomplish the goals of column B, yet a bond can lose value. From 1999 to 2009, if you were holding Lehman Brothers, Bear Stearns, ENRON, or World Com bonds, you might have thought you were safe, but found out just how much you could lose in a bond. If you are holding a California bond right now you might be a little insecure. That is why we use Fixed Principal Assets in column B rather than Fixed Income Assets.

In contrast to bonds, Column B has three Green Money Rules: protect your principal, retain your gains, and guarantee your income. If an asset can't do those three things, it doesn't belong in the ABC Model's Column B. Bonds don't follow those rules so they must go in the next column, column C. Therefore, a Fixed Indexed Annuity is probably an ideal asset for column B."

5.6 **What are some of the negative aspects of annuities you have heard about?**

5.7 **What are some of the positive aspects of annuities you have heard about?**

5.8 **When a planner uses the term "Fixed Income Asset" what do you believe about the primary characteristic of that asset?**

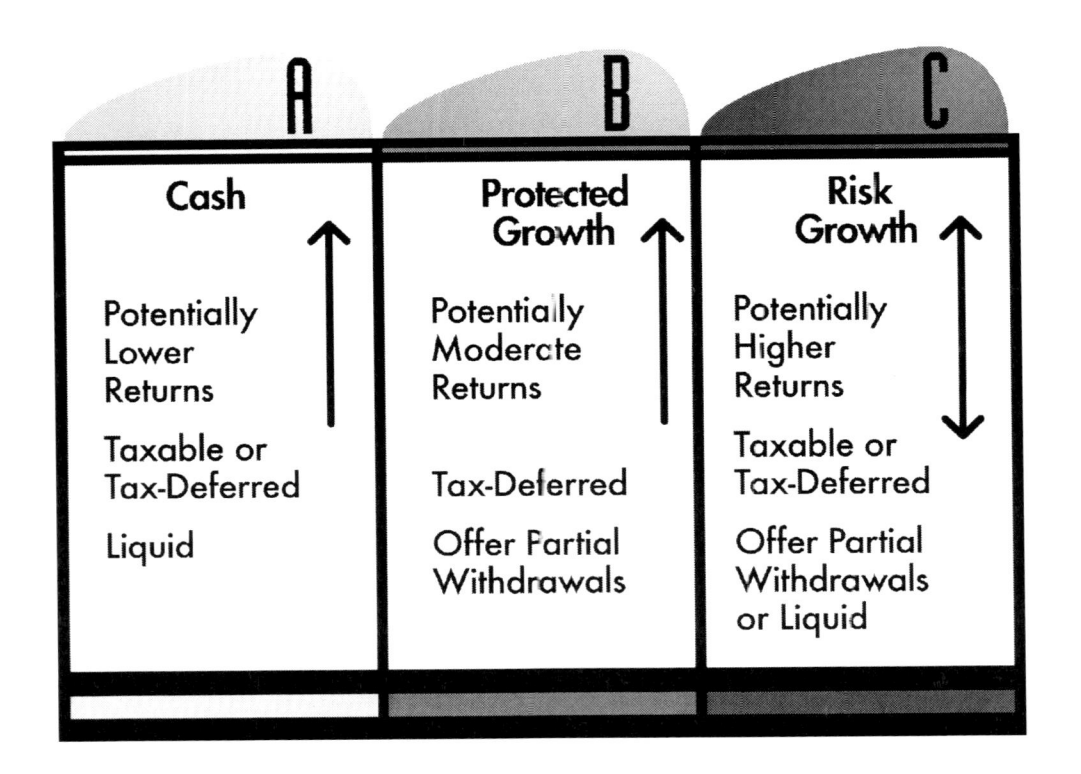

A Cash	**B** Protected Growth	**C** Risk Growth
Potentially Lower Returns ↑	Potentially Moderate Returns ↑	Potentially Higher Returns ↕
Taxable or Tax-Deferred	Tax-Deferred	Taxable or Tax-Deferred
Liquid	Offer Partial Withdrawals	Offer Partial Withdrawals or Liquid

Category C: Risk

"Column C represents our Risk Growth assets, which move up or down with the market. Investors usually chase higher returns over time, though these assets can gain or lose 30% in a year, or even more. The S&P 500 lost 38% in 2008, but the average of 1995-1999 was over 25%. (4) The market "giveth" and the market "taketh" away, there are no protections or limits. This money is invested in securities like stocks, bonds, mutual funds, variable annuities, options, REITs, and the like. The principal isn't protected and last year's gain may be lost in a downturn of the market. While these accounts are associated with a longer time horizon they are usually more liquid due to the "sellable" nature of securities, unless they are in a variable annuity which offers partial withdrawals.

The majority of the assets found in column C are in retirement accounts such as 401(k)'s, 403(b)'s, IRA's, and variable annuities. Column C monies can also be found in the form of non-qualified (after-tax) brokerage accounts, mutual funds, stocks, or bonds, held by an individual, jointly, or even in trust. You can be your own manager or hire a professional investment adviser to manage this part for you. Let's paint these investments Red for Risk."

5.9 What are some of the negative aspects of Column C that concern you as you plan for retirement?

5.10 What are some of the positive aspects of Column C that could help you as you plan for retirement?

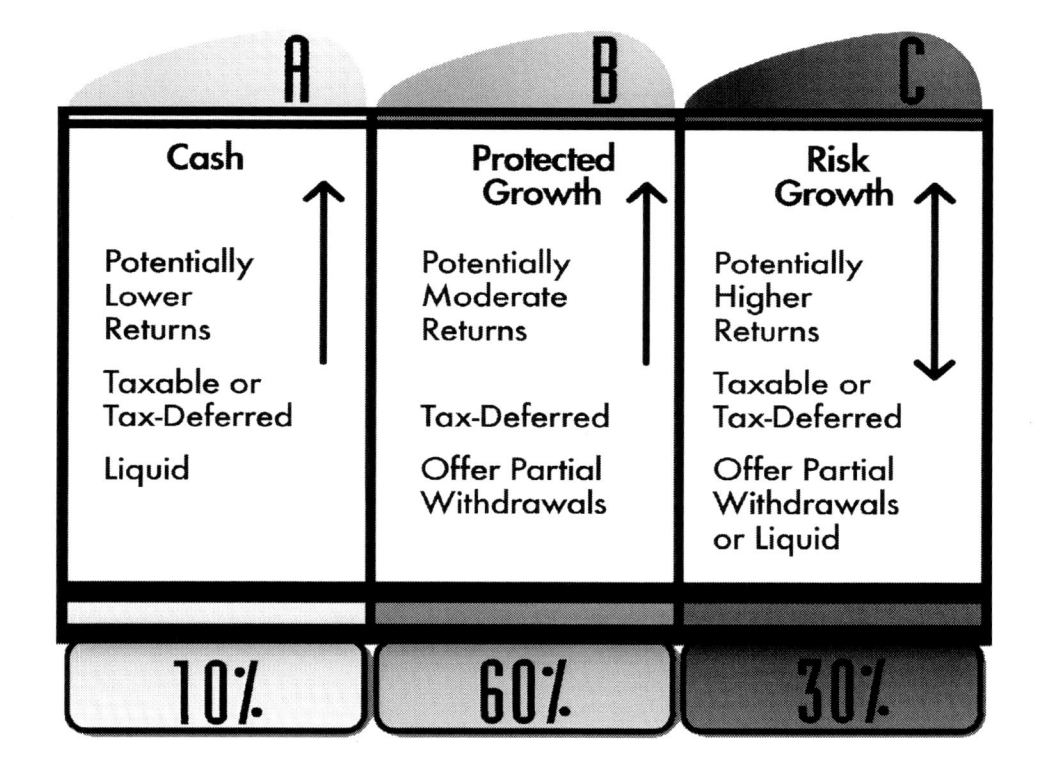

A	B	C
Cash ↑	**Protected Growth** ↑	**Risk Growth** ↕
Potentially Lower Returns	Potentially Moderate Returns	Potentially Higher Returns
Taxable or Tax-Deferred	Tax-Deferred	Taxable or Tax-Deferred
Liquid	Offer Partial Withdrawals	Offer Partial Withdrawals or Liquid
10%	**60%**	**30%**

ABC Example

"If you had $500,000 of investable assets and wanted the 10/60/30 split illustrated above, you would have about $50,000 liquid in bank accounts (Column A), $300,000 in Fixed Index Annuities (Column B), and about $150,000 in securities such as stock mutual funds, bond mutual funds, or managed accounts. When we get to chapter nine, we'll discuss the power of this allocation versus a more growth-oriented portfolio. Needless to say, if the market experienced another 38% drop like in 2008, only 30% of your portfolio would be exposed to a loss. Seventy-percent would not have lost one red penny!"

Create Your Own ABC Model

"So, what percent of your investable assets would you like in each column? Go ahead and take a shot at it.

Start with column (A) and ask yourself how much emergency money or liquidity you need. In other words, don't worry much about returns, but concentrate on liquidity. How much money do you need available immediately? How much money would you need in the next six months to live on if your current income went away? You can express it in a percentage or a specific dollar amount. Your number will be personal to you.

Second, you could ask yourself how much money you want at risk in the market and what type of market risk you want. Do you want Stock-type risk or Bond-type risk? As a conservative investor you probably don't want options or aggressive risk oriented assets. Keep it simple here. Decide how much money you want at risk, and then decide what type of risk. The more conservative you are, the more you will gravitate toward bond-type risk. The more moderate you are, you'll probably have a higher percentage in this column and most of it will be in stock related assets such as mutual funds, ETF's, or managed accounts.

Again, just ask how much money you're willing to expose to losses. If you can't stand the thought of losing a penny, your answer to this question is zero! Go ahead and take a stab at it. Got your number? Let's move on.

Once you have the percentage you want in Columns A and C, simply add them together and subtract from 100 to get your B Column percent. It's that easy. You now have percentages in each column and can make adjustments. For instance, if you feel you have too much at risk simply put more in Columns A or B. Or if you feel you have too much tied up in Column B and don't want any more risk, then simply add more to Column A. Play with the numbers until you think you have what you want."

5.11 **In the box below, put the percentage of your assets you would want to be in each column, to create your own ABC Model.**

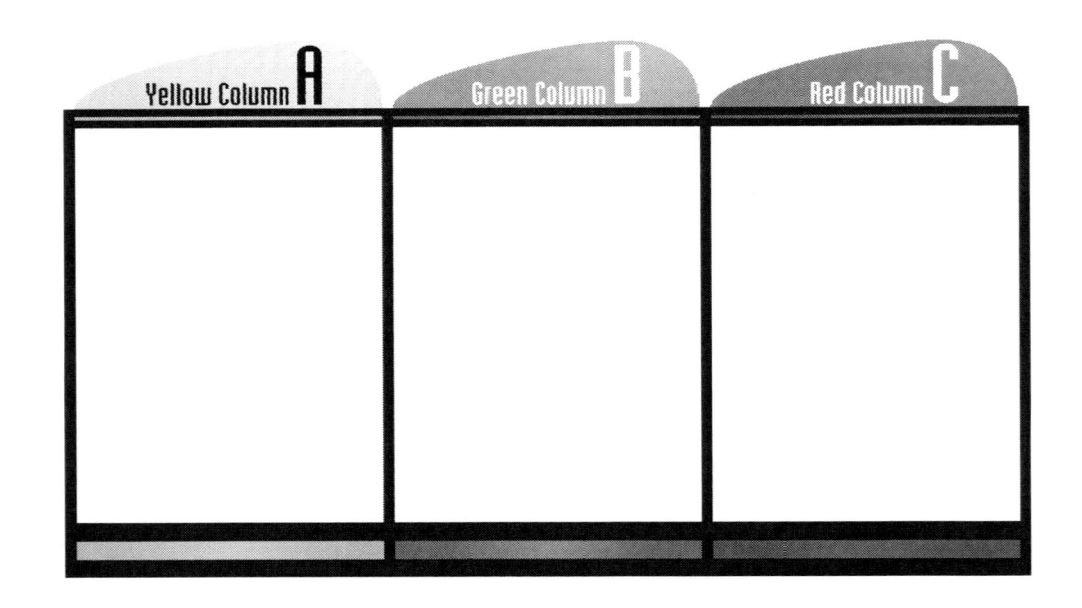

Yellow Column A	Green Column B	Red Column C

Types of Assets

"...column A assets are bank assets such as CD's, money markets, savings accounts, etc. Column B assets are true Fixed Principal Assets. In other words, they are assets where your principal is protected from market fluctuations, and you retain previous years' gains. These would be assets like Fixed Annuities, Fixed Indexed Annuities, and Whole and Universal Life insurance cash values. Column C would contain assets such as stocks, bonds, mutual funds, variable annuities, ETF's, REIT's, hedge funds, Options, etc."

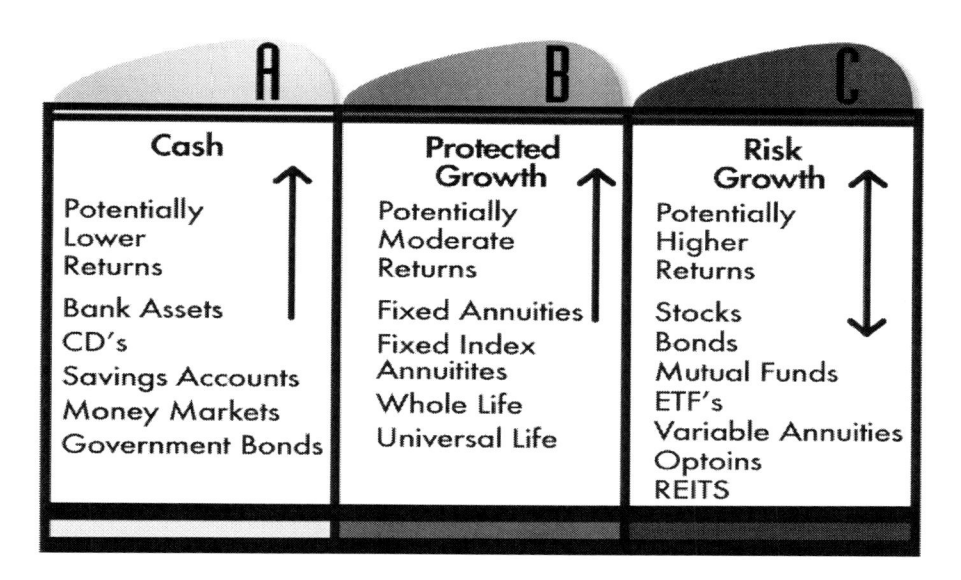

A	B	C
Cash	**Protected Growth**	**Risk Growth**
Potentially Lower Returns	Potentially Moderate Returns	Potentially Higher Returns
Bank Assets	Fixed Annuities	Stocks
CD's	Fixed Index Annuitites	Bonds
Savings Accounts	Whole Life	Mutual Funds
Money Markets	Universal Life	ETF's
Government Bonds		Variable Annuities
		Optoins
		REITS

ABC Risk vs. Reward

"There is a "Risk-Reward" for each column, which means you stand to gain or lose something by placing assets in each scenario… in Column A you give up GAINS to get more LIQUIDITY. In column B you give up some LIQUIDITY to acquire PROTECTION from risk, and in Column C you give up POTECTION for higher potential GAINS, as illustrated below."

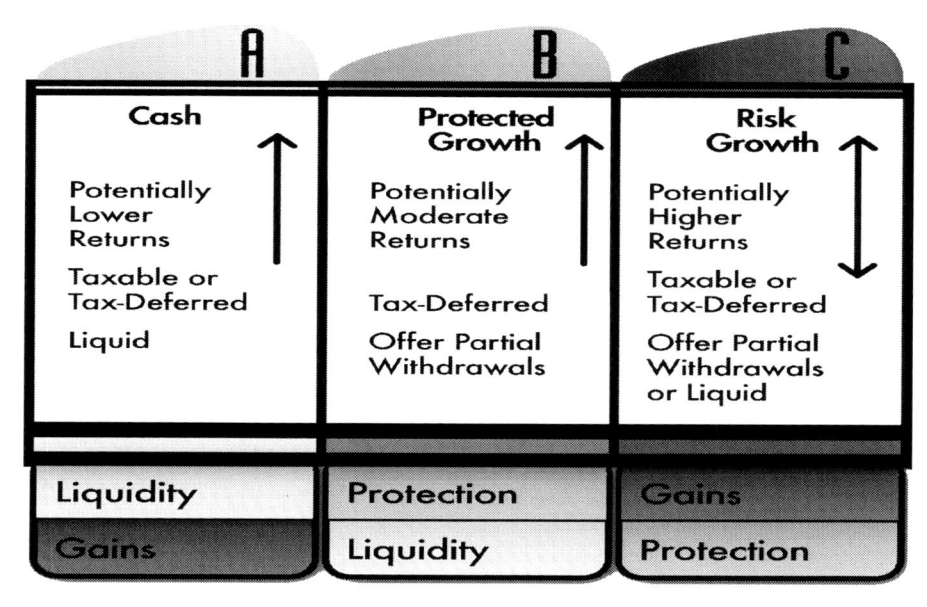

A	B	C
Cash	**Protected Growth**	**Risk Growth**
Potentially Lower Returns	Potentially Moderate Returns	Potentially Higher Returns
Taxable or Tax-Deferred	Tax-Deferred	Taxable or Tax-Deferred
Liquid	Offer Partial Withdrawals	Offer Partial Withdrawals or Liquid
Liquidity	Protection	Gains
Gains	Liquidity	Protection

5.12 How do the "risk-reward" trade-offs impact your planning choices?

Rule of 100

"…you might not have a clue how much money you want in each column and need a little guidance. It might be helpful to picture money as being either GREEN or RED—GREEN for Safe and RED for Risk. GREEN Safe money is money not exposed to risk in the market. RED Risk money is just that, money in the market.

It might also help to picture my friend Steve the Sleepless Investor. He's a 65-year-old retired salesman with $600,000 of investible assets. Steve's advisor suggests an often used formula called the Rule of 100 to help him determine how much he wants in Columns A, B, and C. Very simply he used the formula below of 100 minus his age, to determine how much money he wants in Green protected accounts and Red risk accounts."

RULE OF 100
100
<u>-65</u>   Age
35%   Percent of Red Risk Assets

5.13 Using the rule of 100, what percent of Red Risk Assets would you put in Column C? Explain.

Sleepless Steve

"Steve decides to put 65% in the first two columns. Mr. Sleepless first determines he wants in 10% or $60,000 in Column A for an emergency fund, plus he's planning a "restful" vacation in Seattle. Next, he puts the balance of the green money portion from the Rule of 100 which is 55% or $330,000 in a laddered portfolio of indexed annuities in Column B. Steve has 35% or $210,000 left to be placed in Column C's Red Risk assets. He chooses a professional money manager who manages a conservative portfolio of funds."

Sleepless Steve's ABC Allocation of $600,000

Steve's Rule of **100**
<u>Steve's Age   -65</u>
                35%   Percent of Red Risk Assets

Column A	**Column B**	**Column C**
10%	55%	35%
$60,000	$330,000	$210,000

5.14 Think through your current financial plan. In what ways would this help you re-allocate your portfolio? In what ways would it not help you plan?

5.15 Would you feel comfortable allocating your assets in this manner? Explain.

The Major Differences between Wall Street and the ABC's

"The ABC Model of Investing simply asks you to determine your liquidity needs, and then how much you want at risk. Notice there are two major differences between the ABC Model and Wall Street. First, two out of three categories offer protection of principal. Bank assets are insured by the FDIC. Annuities are backed by the claims paying ability of large insurance carriers. Be sure and ask your agent or broker to inform you about the strength of the insurance companies they recommend. Second, the ABC's are easier for the average person to understand which gives the conservative investor confidence.

Protection and simplicity are keys in the ABC's. Yes, there is an allotment for Red Risk money, and the ABC Model makes it easy to determine how much risk a conservative desires. In the next three chapters, we'll discuss in detail each category's investments."

5.16 **In what ways would the ABC Planning Model help you in your financial planning?**

Chapter Five Notes

FINANCIAL ABC's
of retirement planning

Chapter Six

Who's the King?
Yellow Money Savings

The Goal of Yellow Money

"The goal of Column A, Yellow Money, is to provide a sufficient amount of liquidity for the majority of your portfolio while keeping it protected from losses due to fluctuations in the stock market. Remember, yellow money is money that typically earns lower returns, is guaranteed by FDIC, and can be liquidated with minimal expense and maximum efficiency. We are not expecting big gains in these assets because this is "cash." As a rule, the longer the time horizon for an investment, the greater the potential returns. When people say that money never sleeps, they're wrong. This money is fast asleep, earning very little, but is available and free from market risk.

You also want to have cash available in the event you can't work for six months to a year. You don't have to keep 6-12 month's salary available however you do want to have your basic living expenses covered. For example, if your monthly expenses total $2,500 and you wanted to cover six months, then you would need $15,000 in Yellow money accounts. If you wanted to cover a twelve-month budget at this rate you would need $30,000. In order to get the most interest, you could make use of CD's that mature after six to twelve months and ladder their maturities."

6.1 **What are some items you might have to plan for on a short term basis, in the range of 12-18 months?**

"The reason you want to have Yellow money available for these short time-frame events is that you don't want to have to sell off long-term assets when they may be at a loss because of market fluctuations or early redemption penalties."

How much liquidity?

6.2 Put a dollar figure on how much liquidity is right for you?

6.3 It's often helpful to develop a budget in order to see these items more clearly. Fill out the sample budget worksheet found in Appendix 2.

"At any rate, you will want to determine either a dollar figure or a percentage of assets allotted for Column A giving you the liquidity and safety you desire. For instance, say you have $700,000 of investible assets."

Two Yellow Money Categories

It's helpful to know Yellow money can be divided easily into two categories:
1. Accessible with **no penalties** for early withdrawal
    a. Checking accounts
    b. FDIC insured money markets
    c. Savings accounts
2. Accessible with **minimal penalties** for early withdrawal
    a. CD's
    b. Government Savings Bonds, i.e. EE bonds, H bonds, etc.

Accessible with no penalties for withdrawal

"First on the list are checking accounts that banks and other savings institutions offer. While these are the most easily accessed funds, they are also the least profitable. They usually come with fees attached and no interest, though banks offer some interest-bearing accounts with the caveat of a high minimum balance. It's often wise to keep only your monthly cash needs in your checking accounts due to low interest.

Next you have FDIC Insured Money Markets that traditionally pay a higher amount of interest, yet still have checkbook access. It's important to note that not all money market accounts are FDIC insured and thus exposed to fluctuations in value, though usually minor."

"A common practice suggested by financial planners is to have all your general deposits, including pensions, social security, and automated deposits pour into your money market account. Then you can transfer enough money for your monthly bills out of the money market in to your checking account. Because the money market account usually receives higher interest, it assures your largest cash account receives the most amount of interest."

"Finally, we have bank savings accounts generally paying somewhere between money market and checking account rates. These accounts do not usually have checking privileges and are being used less and less."

6.4 **What do you think of the author's idea of all deposits going to a money market and only transferring enough cash for monthly expenses into your checking account?**

Accessible with minimal penalties for early withdrawal

"First on the list of accessible assets that carry a minimal penalty for early withdrawal are Certificates of Deposit, or CDs as they are commonly referred to. CDs are the preferred yellow money savings vehicle of many retired Americans. The reasons are obvious. They can provide a modest rate of return while maturing at relatively short periods. The rates are determined by the banking institution and declared in advance."

"CD rates have adjusted over the years with lows in 2009 under 1% APR to the early 1980's rates of 12%-18% APR.(1)… you may have to wait a long time before rates are in the double digits again."

"It's important to realize that CD interest is taxable each year. In other words, if you made 2% on your $100,000 last year, you would be adding the $2,000 you made to your income tax whether you take out the interest or not. That income may affect your tax bracket, social security taxation, and possibly your real estate tax, depending on the state you live in. It's kind of like "good news, bad news." You made $2,000 more, but it forced you into a higher tax bracket, made you pay taxes on 85% of your social security instead of 50%, and you lost the real estate tax exemption on your home."

"The last assets we look at in Column A are government savings bonds like EE and HH bonds. They really don't have a penalty for early withdrawal other than losing the full potential of the asset at maturity. Once you liquidate the bond you will have to pay taxes on the interest you received over the course of holding the bond. Savings bonds are different than CD's in that you don't pay taxes on the interest until you liquidate the bond. You could hold the bond 30 years and not pay interest until the end. The interest is included as income on your tax return in the year you liquidate. The good news is you made money, and the bad news is you owe Uncle Sam because you made money. While not very practical because they are cumbersome to liquidate, they are as safe an asset as you can get. These bonds typically offer lower interest rates."

6.5 **What other benefits or drawbacks to having government bonds might there be?**

Savings, not Investing

"...the regulators look at cash accounts such as CD's, savings accounts, checking accounts, and FDIC-insured money markets, as savings vehicles not investments. That's because the only risk involved is interest rate risk, or the risk that you would have to hold a CD at 2% while others are being issued at 3%. While your principal is protected up to the FDIC limit, you are said to have "deposited" money in a savings instrument rather than "invested" money in a security."

6.6   Is having the majority of your money liquid important to you? Why or why not?

"Some people believe they need all their money liquid all the time. Just think about that for a minute. If you had the $700,000 mentioned in the example above, would you really need all of it accessible at any moment? This is a common mistake amongst highly conservative investors. It is a method of investing that will lend itself to diminishing your buying power over time because of low rates not keeping up with inflation. Don't make this mistake. As you'll see in the next chapter, you can still have protection, but with potentially higher average returns."

Chapter Six Notes

FINANCIAL ABC's
of retirement planning

Chapter Seven

"They Are Who We Thought They Were"[1]
Green Money Premium

Fixed Income Asset or Fixed Principal Asset?

"In the investing community, the term Fixed Income Asset can refer to a number of financial vehicles like Asset Backed Securities and even Derivatives. The most common Fixed Income Asset is a Bond. This illustrates how disconnected Wall Street is from Main Street. When Wall Street uses the term Fixed Income Asset, the average person believes their principal is guaranteed. In fact, a bond IS a fixed income asset because the phrase refers to the "income" being fixed. However, people don't hear "fixed income," they hear "fixed" and believe their principal is protected when in reality it isn't.

This may come as a surprise to some, but bonds can lose value. Just ask those who held ENRON bonds, WorldCom bonds, Lehman Brothers, or Bear Stearns bonds. If you are holding California bonds you might be just a little nervous, too. You are told that if you hold the bond till maturity you will get your money back. There are NO GUARANTEES!

Choosing the right assets for Column B is crucial to a balanced, conservative portfolio. Assets should have what you think they should have, if you choose the right ones. You should gain security through the one element most investors think of when they hear the word "fixed" as it relates to an asset, which is protection of your principal. So, let's use the term Fixed Principal Asset to describe the financial vehicles we will use in Column B."

7.1 Do you know anyone who has lost money in bonds?

7.2 In the past, have you thought bonds guaranteed principal? Explain.

Three Green Money Rules for Choosing Assets in Column B

Green Money Rule #1: Protect Your Principal

Any asset in this category must have protection of principal if you follow the asset's rules. In other words, if you stay to term you must be guaranteed your principal in return.

Green Money Rule #2: Retain Your Gains

Over the contract term any gains you receive in this asset class are secured, unless of course you decide to withdraw the dollars and spend them.

Green Money Rule #3: Guarantee Your Income

Assets in Column B must have the ability to guarantee income in some manner.

> "It's a common misconception amongst investors that Bonds would fit in Column B. They don't. The reason is simple. There are no bonds that obey all three Green Money Rules! They are not who we thought they were! Bonds belong in Column C.
>
> There is an asset that obeys all three rules. It is a Fixed Indexed Annuity (FIA) or even just a Fixed Annuity. An Indexed Annuity is a contract with an insurance company for an income, funded by an initial premium, whose interest is linked in some manner to an index in the stock or bond market. Principal is guaranteed, gains are retained, and an income stream is guaranteed in the form of an annuity payment or guaranteed withdrawal benefits."

7.3 **How do the Green Money Rules help when forming a balanced, conservative portfolio?**

What is an Annuity?

> "An annuity, technically, is a contract with an insurance company for an income payment either now or in the future. The word annuity means "payment." It's all about the payments to you! If the payment is now, the annuity is called an "immediate annuity." If the income payment to you is in the future, then the annuity is called a "deferred annuity" because the payment is deferred. It can be a Single Premium Deferred Annuity (SPDA) or a Flexible Premium Deferred Annuity (FPDA). You can purchase the annuity with a single lump sum as in a SPDA or make premium payments in a FPDA. By the way, they call the deposits into an annuity "premiums" because you are purchasing a guaranteed payment. They don't call them deposits as in a Certificate of Deposit or an investment as in a stock or mutual fund.
>
> For our purposes in Column B Green Money strategies, we will only be talking about Deferred Annuities. Remember, this is an annuity where your payment from the insurance company is deferred until you choose to receive it."

Variable Annuities

"…the variable annuity puts the risk of the principal on the investor, while the fixed annuity puts the risk on the insurance company.

When you purchase a variable annuity, your premiums go into a fund at the insurance company. The company offers you the option to choose from a varied amount of side accounts which are much like mutual funds. In fact, though they are not technically mutual funds, they are managed by the same managers and are after the same results. You might have portfolio options like American Funds, T. Rowe Price, Janus, Fidelity, ING, etc. They would typically give you a range of fund strategies from Growth to Value, and Emerging Markets to Domestic, and even some Bond Funds. You will pay management fees inside these funds along with other fees and expenses typical of variable annuities. These expenses range from 1.25% to 5% depending on the amount options you choose for your variable annuity.

For instance, you will always have what's called a Mortality and Expense Fee (M&E) of around 1.15% to 1.5%. These fees pay for the death benefit and general expenses inside the annuity that an insurance company incurs. Add to that an enhanced death benefit that guarantees not only your deposit, but increases your benefit to heirs in some manner. The cost varies, but might be .75%. Then you might want to choose a popular guaranteed income option or withdrawal benefit. These options might cost an additional .75%. If you add up where we are so far it looks like this:

M&E Charges	1.25%
Enhanced Death Benefit	.75%
Income Benefit	.75%
Fund Management Fees	.65%
Total	3.4%

You can see how these expenses might add up rather quickly as they provide increasing benefits. Also, because it's a variable annuity, your account statements will fluctuate and you can lose principal. Your potential for a higher gain than a traditional fixed annuity is greater, yet your exposure is more significant."

"…it is definitely not a Column B Green Money Asset. It breaks Rule #1, Protect Your Principal. So, if you are going to use it, you should think of it as a Column C Red Money asset."

While variable annuities are a risk oriented asset they can also provide some income and death benefit protections that other securities can't.

7.4 In what ways might it be an advantage to use a variable annuity in your portfolio?

7.5 In what ways might a variable annuity be a disadvantage in your portfolio?

Fixed & Fixed Indexed Annuities

"Cleary then, the main characteristic of a Fixed Annuity is the protection of your principal. How then does a fixed annuity gain in value? Unlike a Variable Annuity, a Fixed Annuity guarantees principal and credits interest to your account, normally on an annual basis. It's this interest crediting that separates traditional fixed annuities from fixed indexed annuities.

"The insurance company in a traditional fixed annuity announces the interest it will credit for the year in advance, much like a bank announces its interest rate on CD's. It is compounded and tax-deferred. The subtle contrast in an indexed annuity is how the company determines the amount of interest to credit. An indexed annuity's interest rate is tied to an index such as the S&P 500. If the index goes up, the owner of the annuity is credited with a portion of the increase in the index and those gains are retained in the contract. If the index goes down, both the principal and previous years gains are retained, and the owner of the annuity loses no ground."

Four Year FIA Graph

Below is a four year graph illustrating a basic fixed indexed annuity (FIA). Notice at the bottom of the illustration there are some additional aspects of an FIA to be sure and cover with your agent. Each insurance company structures the annuities differently and there are many options to choose from.

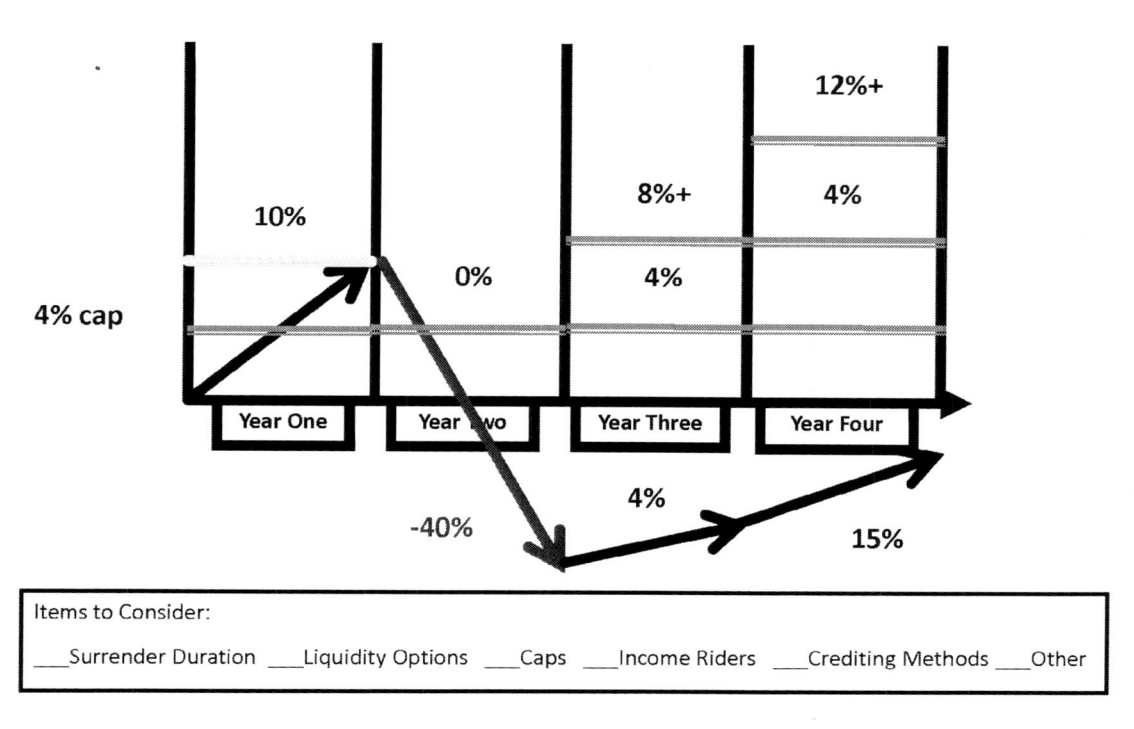

Items to Consider:
___Surrender Duration   ___Liquidity Options   ___Caps   ___Income Riders   ___Crediting Methods   ___Other

7.6 How does the structure of an Indexed Annuity protect your principal and retain your gains?

7.7 In the illustration above, would you be upset with a "0" in year two? Why or Why not?

7.8 In the illustration above, would you want a greater return in year 4 when the market rose 15%? Explain.

What are the FIA Guarantees?

"Fixed Indexed annuities are guaranteed by the issuing insurance company who provides a contractually stated guarantee in each annuity. Insurance companies offer a minimum guaranteed return by using a 1%-3% interest rate on a portion of the initial premium for the duration of the contract. This enables the contract holder to receive their premium back at the end of the surrender period. Usually, the insurance company uses something less than 100% of the principal upon which to credit the minimum interest. For example, an insurance company might credit a minimum of 2% on 87% of the premium, as seen below."

FIA Guarantee Example:
Premium $100,000
87% of Premium $87,000
Minimum Interest   2%
Number of Contract Years   10
Minimum Guaranteed Balance $106,053

"...The insurance company assumes the risk of the asset in the fixed indexed annuity, while the investor holds all the risk with a variable annuity.

It's also important to note that insurance companies are regulated by the State Insurance Departments of each state, not the Securities and Exchange Commission. Company's investments and business practices are under the very watchful eyes of the State Insurance Commissioners."

7.9 How important to you are the guarantees on annuities? Explain.

How Does an FIA Credit Interest?

"Indexed Annuities have a wide range of options the contract owner can select from to link the interest rate to the market. These options are called "crediting methods" and can usually be changed annually. The owner of the contract selects which crediting option or options they want to use each year, deciding what percent of the total account value to put into each crediting method. Somewhere around the anniversary date, the insurance company allows the owner to change the allotment of values in the crediting options."

Below is a sample from the book of Index Annuity crediting methods:

Fixed Rate – Indexed annuities usually carry an option of a one year fixed interest rate. They announce the rate each year and also have a minimum guaranteed rate this strategy can never go under.

S&P 500 Annual Point to Point with a Cap – In this method, the interest is tied to the S&P 500 for the contract year and is given a cap on how much interest can be credited. The "point" referred to is the anniversary date of the contract. So, between the first anniversary date (point #1) and twelve months later (point #2), the insurance company looks at how the S&P 500 performed.

For example, if the market moved 10% in a year with a 5% Cap you would receive a 5% interest credit. In other words you would get 100% of the upward movement in the market up to 5%. If the market goes up 5% you get 5%. If it goes up 20% you get 5%. It's important to note that caps can change and they usually come with contractual minimum guaranteed caps. For instance, the lowest cap the insurance company can use for the year might be 1.5%.

One of the most attractive features of this type of indexed crediting is the company will reset the point at where the annuity calculates the interest each year. So, if the S&P 500 Index was at 1000 on your first anniversary date, the company would use that number as the starting point to figure that year's interest. If the index finished the year below 1000, say 850, your annuity would "reset" the starting point to 850 and calculate from there for the following year. In that way you are only looking at individual anniversary years rather than trying to beat the annuity's first year starting point five years down the road. This function is called "annual reset" and works in the favor of the contract holder.

Imagine if you didn't have this feature in your indexed annuity, and had to rely on a ten-year window. If that had happened from 2000 to 2010 you would have had virtually no gain in your asset! So, annual reset or even bi-annual reset is an incredible feature.

S&P 500 Annual Point to Point with a Participation Rate – This option is a take on the first method, but instead of using a cap the company will issue a rate at which your contract can "participate" in the gain of the market. So, if you have a 50% participation rate and the market went up 10%, you would receive 5%, if it went up 20% you would receive 10%. Again the insurance company has a minimum guaranteed participation rate at which they can never go lower.

S&P 500 Monthly Point to Point with a Cap – Here is a variation of annual point to point with the insurance company looking at individual months to determine the gain in your contract rather than years. The company will issue a cap on each month at the beginning of the contract year. They will then look at each month individually, adding them up at the end of the year to determine the rate of return. It is important to know that the Cap is an "upside" cap. There is no downside cap. Let me illustrate. Assuming a monthly cap of 2% let's look at a 12-month cycle:

S&P Monthly Point to Point with Cap Example:

Contract Month	S&P500 Return	Annuity Percent
1	2%	2%
2	3%	2%
3	1%	1%
4	-3%	-3%
5	0%	0%
6	-1%	-1%
7	1%	1%
8	2%	2%
9	5%	2%
10	1%	1%
11	3%	2%
12	0%	0%
Total	14%	9%

Notice in the graph above that in months 2, 9, and 11 the market went up more than 2% and the annuity was only credited with the 2%. Actually, it wasn't credited during the year. The company waits to total the numbers until the end of the year and then credit the interest to the contract. In year 4 the market went down more than the 2% cap and the whole negative number was put into the equation. If this ever created a situation where at the end of the year the total was negative, the annuity would get 0%. This is good if the market actually had a down year and you didn't lose anything, yet it can also create a lower return in a year that has a significant volatility between the months that wipes out gains for the year. This method has the potential to credit much higher gains in a market trending upward, but can create zeros in volatile years. When the market has a down year, Zero is your Hero!

S&P 500 Monthly Average with a Cap or Participation Rate - As illustrated with the first two crediting methods, this method uses a cap and/or a participation rate. Yet, different from the monthly point to point, it averages the twelve months between anniversaries. If the market is really hot in the first three quarters yet suffers losses in the last quarter, this method saves the year. Very simply, the insurance company keeps a record of the percentages of the movement in the market on a monthly basis, then divides by 12, applies the cap or participation rate for the final result. This is historically the least effective method.

Multi-Year with a Mix of Interest and a Percentage of the Market – One of the great innovations in the indexed annuity business is the invention of a new multi-year strategy that combines a percentage of the market with an interest rate. This is one of the few index annuities that charge a fee, but the fee is different than the fees on a variable annuity. The difference is the variable annuity charges fees regardless of annual performance and is on the entire account value. This indexed annuity has fees only on the gain in the annuity. If there's no gain there's no fee. The back testing on these types of annuities has been very promising. They are popular because of their innovation and fewer moving parts.

While Multi-Year annuities don't make use of an "annual reset" feature, they usually offer a two to five year reset period. Purchasing two to five year options in the market are generally less expensive than shorter term options. Thus the insurance company has the ability to pass through more interest to the contract holder.

Other crediting methods include the use of additional indexes such as the Dow Jones Industrial Index, Russell 2000, S&P MidCap 400, EuroDow, Hang Seng (China) Index, US Treasury, Barclay's Aggregate Bond Index, as examples. Companies use one, two, and three year monthly point to point strategies, multi-year monthly averaging, high water mark, and vesting schedules as alternatives for crediting methods. An excellent resource for researching crediting methods is Jack Marrion's website www.IndexAnnuity.org. He lists various companies and their current rates."

7.10   Which of the crediting methods most appeal to you?

Any Fees in FIA's?

"…the cost is accounted for internally within the insurance company in most cases. Some of the newer versions of multi-year crediting methods come with fees on the gains as mentioned above, but other than that the only fees associated with indexed annuities are related to added benefits such as income riders. There are no mortality and expense fees or enhanced death benefit fees in most index annuities."

"First, the money you put into an indexed annuity with an insurance company is generally invested in high grade bonds, mostly government bonds. These bonds pay an interest rate to the insurance company. Let's say the bond yields 6%. The insurance company takes a portion of the interest for its profit and expenses and then there is what's called "excess interest.

In an indexed annuity, the excess interest is invested in call options in the market index related to the annuity crediting method chosen. Call options are contracts that give the holder the right to buy a security at a specified time in the future. The call option is valuable if the security it's tied to goes up and worthless if it goes down in the contracted time frame. This process allows the insurance carrier to build in profit, pay for costs such as an agent, and provide an attractive benefit to the contract holder."

7.11   Before now did you believe all annuities, even fixed annuities, had fees? Explain.

How About Liquidity?

"If the benefit of an indexed annuity is a potential for a higher gain than other fixed assets then the drawback is its long term nature. In order for the insurance company to create a win-win situation for themselves and the client, the money has to stay put for a while so the underlying investments have time to work the way they are designed. This is the reason that annuity companies have surrender penalties associated with early withdrawals. These surrender penalties usually decline on an annual basis, say over a 5 to 10 year period. There are annuities with longer surrender periods.

Remember, these penalties are for any monies liquidated in excess of the penalty free withdrawal options or for total early withdrawal. Early withdrawal means you might have had an annuity with ten years of declining surrender penalties and totally liquidated in the third year, thus creating a penalty. A ten-year declining surrender period might start with a ten percent penalty in the first year and decline one percent a year for ten years. In the eleventh year you could withdraw all the money in your annuity without any penalty."

"…most indexed annuities have the ability for the contract holder to withdraw 10% of the cash value on an annual basis through penalty free withdrawals. The companies also provide the availability for annuity payment options at certain points over the contract years. That means you can turn the asset into a guaranteed income stream that you can't outlive."

7.12 Compare an Indexed Annuity's liquidity to other assets?

"Indexed annuities are not only moderately liquid, but most make provisions in the contract that allow for more than the ten percent penalty-free withdrawals in the event of long-term care needs, disability, or terminal illness. In most cases these provisions allow you to withdraw 100% of your money before the contract term is over without any penalties."

Laddered Maturities in FIA's

"…indexed annuities are long term in nature and carry early withdrawal penalties. Laddering the surrender years can create liquidity in the portfolio over time.

"To illustrate, let's assume you wanted to allocate $300,000 in Column B. You could have five annuities with $60,000 in each one, starting with an annuity that has five years of surrender penalties and ending with a ten year annuity. You could even get bonuses in some of the annuities. That's right, bonuses!

Insurance companies will offer bonuses for monies that stay longer in the contract. For instance, you can get an 8% immediate bonus on your account in a ten year annuity. If you put the $60,000 in, the first day it becomes $64,800 and any interest for that year is compounded on top of that figure."

"Here's an example of a laddered maturity of five index annuities using hypothetical insurance companies:

1. XYZ Insurance Company – **5 Years**
2. Integrity Insurance Company – **6 Years**
3. American Insurance Company – **7 Years**
4. Super Life & Annuity Company with a 3% Bonus – **8 Years**
5. Big Daddy Insurance Company with an 8% Bonus – **10 Years**"

"…if you wanted to create greater liquidity at a faster rate you could use larger amounts in the shortest term annuities and smaller amounts with the longest annuities."

Examples

The following illustrates a $500,000 account divided into five $100,000 premium deposits in five different companies' annuities with sequential terms starting at 5 years to 10 years, and assumes an average 4% average rate of return. "At term" below refers to the time in the annuity contract when there are no longer any surrender penalties for withdrawal of funds.

1. *Five year* annuity becomes $121,665 at term
2. *Six year* annuity becomes $126,532 at term
3. *Seven year* annuity becomes $131,593 at term
4. *Eight year with 3% Bonus* annuity becomes $140,963 at term
5. *Ten year with 8% Bonus* annuity becomes $159,866 at term

Using this example, having put $100,000 in the annuity in the first year, after five years its cash value is totally liquid, without penalty. The same happens for the six year annuity and so on until all is liquid in the tenth year. Remember, most annuities also offer 10% penalty free withdrawals of the entire cash account value each year after the first year.

Here is an example using an assumed a 5% growth:

1. *Five year* annuity becomes $127,628 at term
2. *Six year* annuity becomes $134,010 at term
3. *Seven year* annuity becomes $140,710 at term
4. *Eight year with 3% Bonus* annuity becomes $152,178 at term
5. *Ten year with 8% Bonus* annuity becomes $175,921 at term

As you can see, using laddered maturities of index annuities offers the conservative planner a high degree of security along with moderate liquidity.

"The following is a comparison for planning using a ladder vs. not using a ladder:

Planning without a Ladder
- Usually one long term annuity
- Lack of liquidity
- Crediting methods of only one company
- Safety related to only one company
- No diversity in performance or management
- Larger commissions for the agents

Planning with a Ladder
- Multiple shorter term annuities
- Liquidity develops over years
- Diverse crediting methods by various companies
- Safety of multiple companies
- Diversity in performance and management
- Smaller average commissions for agents"

7.13 **What advantages or disadvantages do you see in using a laddered maturity of Indexed Annuities?**

Planning for Income with an Indexed Annuity

"Income guarantees are the latest phase of indexed annuity innovation. Companies seem to be coming out with new guaranteed income or withdrawal benefits every month."

"Basically, there are two ways to get money out of an annuity. You either "annuitize" or "withdraw." The major difference is what happens to the account value when you choose either of these two options. You could probably understand annuitization best if you think of it as a pension payment. When you retire from a company, sometimes you are offered a choice between a lump sum and a monthly payment. If you take the lump sum, you receive a one-time cash payment of your retirement benefits from that company, and typically you invest it to create the income you desire. Yet, if you opt for the pension payments your company will send you a monthly check for the rest of your life or for the rest of you and your spouse's lives in some manner."

7.14 **What happens to the cash value at your company when you choose a pension payment?**

"You can receive payments guaranteed in various manners from an annuity. A common falsehood propagated by an uneducated press is once you choose payments from an annuity company and die, say after just two payments, the company will keep the rest of your money. While this is one option in an annuity contract (called "life only"), it is certainly not the only option and is definitely the least used for obvious reasons."

"You can choose a joint-life option for you and your wife, which creates a payment for the both of you until...well, you know... you expire. You can even choose to have a certain amount of years guaranteed in addition to payments for the rest of your life. For example, you may want to guarantee payments for the first 10 years to you or your heirs. If you lived past the ten years, you would receive payments for as long as you live. You could guarantee payments for not only the first 10 years, but 15, 20, or more years. This method is called "life with a ten-year certain" or "20-year certain and life." Keep in mind that the more you have the company guarantee, the smaller the payments. That's why "life only" payments get chosen because they are usually the highest dollar amount."

Guaranteed Withdrawal Benefits

"…probably the cutting edge of annuity development are the "Guaranteed Income Benefits" or "Guaranteed Withdrawal Benefits." These offer the best of both worlds, the availability of your cash account to stay liquid and a guaranteed income stream. Here's how it works.

First, you need to understand that insurance companies have the ability to account for the money in your contract in various ways, at the same time. Here are a few examples of accounts in a typical indexed annuity:

- **Accumulation Value**
  The current value of your annuity's cash account which includes any bonus and all interest credits to date, less any withdrawals.

- **Income Account Value**
  The current value of your annuity's income account which includes any bonus and all interest credits to date, less any withdrawals. Note: there is no cash value here.

- **Current Surrender Value**
  The current value of your annuity's cash account which includes any bonus and all interest credits to date, less any withdrawals, and minus any surrender charges that would apply if you chose to liquidate.

- **Guaranteed Minimum Surrender Value**
  The current value of your annuity's cash account which includes any bonus and the *minimum guaranteed* interest credits to date, less any withdrawals, and minus any surrender charges that would apply if you chose to liquidate."

7.15 **What are the two main differences between the Accumulation Value and the Income Account Value?**

"An insurance company utilizing a guaranteed withdrawal benefit (GWB) offers a rider, (an amendment to your contract), which you can choose to accept or reject. These riders come with fees so you surely want the option to choose. The rider has two elements. It comes with a guaranteed interest rate and a guaranteed withdrawal percentage. The interest rate is credited to your initial premium and bonus each year for a declared number of years. This interest rate will increase your "income account value" only, and not your "accumulation value." In other words, it is not for cash value growth, but rather calculates the account value from which you may withdraw a guaranteed amount.

The withdrawal percentage is also guaranteed in your rider. It may range from 3% to 7%, depending on your age. In other words, you are guaranteed a lifetime of withdrawals based on the percentage stated at the age you choose to start withdrawals. For instance, the guaranteed income account growth rate might be 6.5%, and if you were to withdraw funds starting at age 70 you would be able to withdraw 5% of the accrued value. Some companies now offer inflation protection on the withdrawals, increasing them by 3% per year or some other formula for the growth of the withdrawal. Typically the withdrawal percentages increase with age, as illustrated below, and are different for each company:

Guaranteed Withdrawal Percentage:
Ages 60 – 69   4-5%
Ages 70 – 79   5-6%
Ages 80 & up   6-7%

Let's combine the guaranteed growth rate and the guaranteed withdrawal percent to see how it works:

Guaranteed Withdrawal Benefit (GWB) Example:
Guaranteed Income Account Growth Rate: 6.5%
Bonus: 8%
Premium: $100,000
Age at Issue: 60
Age Withdrawals Chosen: 70
Guaranteed Withdrawal Percent: 6%
Income Account Value: $202,731
Guaranteed Annual Withdrawal Benefit: $12,164

The $12,164 annual withdrawal is guaranteed for life, no matter what happens to the accumulation value, which by the way would continue to earn interest credits attached to the indexes chosen. In order to match this feat, you would have to find an asset that returned a shade over 7.7% every year for the rest of your life, assuming a 15% net tax rate! That's the incredible power of a guaranteed withdrawal benefit"

7.16   In what ways would you see a GWB enhancing your retirement strategies?

7.17   How would you explain the Green Money Column B to a friend?

Disclosure: Past performance is no guarantee future results. Crediting rates including caps for FIA's can change and are determined by the insurance companies at the time of issue. Future performance cannot be predicted or guaranteed. FIA's are not registered as a security with the SEC and is not invested directly in any stock, bond, or security investment. FIA products, features, and benefits vary by state.

Annuity Contracts are products of the insurance industry and are not guaranteed by any bank or insured by the FDIC. When purchasing a fixed indexed annuity, you own an annuity contract backed by the insurance company, you are not purchasing shares of stocks or indexes. Product features such as interest rates, caps, and participation rates may vary by product and state and may be subject to change. Surrender charges may apply for early withdrawals. Be sure to review the specific product disclosure for more details. Guarantees are based on the financial strength and claims paying ability of the insurance company.

This information is not intended to give tax, legal, or investment advice. Please seek advice from a qualified professional on these matters.

Lifetime income benefit riders are used to calculate lifetime payments only. The income account value is not available for cash surrender or in a death benefit. Excess withdrawals may reduce lifetime income and may incur surrender charges. Fees may apply. Guarantees based on the financial strength and claims paying ability of the insurance company. See specific product disclosure for more details.

Chapter Seven Notes

Chapter Eight

How's the Weather?
Red Money Planning

"Red Money investing relies on forecasts, past correlations, analytical studies, common sense, and a little luck. If you are counting on fair weather, you may just get a hurricane instead. Red Money investing is where the weather of risk changes constantly. Column C is the only place where the clouds of market risk could blow in or the unseasonable heat and humidity of volatility might flare up."

8.1 **If you haven't done so already, now would be a good time to take the Risk Tolerance Questionnaire found in Appendix 3.**

Systematic Risk, Volatility, & Variance
(Now there's a mouthful!)

"…it is important to have a working knowledge of the basic terms used when investing Red Risk Money…let's start with a few words you might have heard a broker say or an analyst use on a financial program.

First, when I say "the market" I'm referring to either the stock market or bond market as a whole. The stock market may be represented by an index such as the S&P 500 and the bond market by the Barclays Capital Aggregate Bond Index. The stock market is sometimes referred to as the equity markets where the average person can own a piece of the store. The bond market, which is the larger of the two, is where debt obligations are sold. A debt obligation is a note issued by an entity such as a corporation or governing body. The bond is guaranteed by the issuer who promises to pay interest on a regular basis. Thus we have stock-type risk and bond-type risk—two aspects of risk in the market as a whole.

Indexes like the S&P 500, Dow Jones Industrials, Russell 2000, Barclays Aggregate Bond Index to name a few, are used to measure the changes in the financial markets. Indexes are referred to as benchmarks against which mutual funds and other investments are measured. They use a theoretical portfolio of assets that are relative to the financial market or economy being measured. You can't actually invest in an index, but index mutual funds, futures and exchange traded funds are used by investors who want to buy into the market as a whole or a particular segment of the market.

Wall Street calls the risk or uncertainty associated with the entire market, or an entire segment of a market, "systematic risk." (1) In other words, investing in the market in general is uncertain all the time. There is never a point at which you can say you know where the market is headed. In fact, systematic risk implies that uncertainty is deep-seated in the market which moves up and down with regularity that cannot be anticipated."

8.2　How does "systematic risk" make you feel?

"How Wall Street measures risk associated with the market is through "volatility." People who study the market look at historical returns of a stock or index and plot them on a graph. They look to see how the dots on the graph relate to each other over time and in relationship to historical events. The further apart the dots on the graph, the higher the volatility. The higher the volatility, the riskier the investment.

Wall Street uses "variance" to describe the difference between where the returns are from an average return of the same asset or a corresponding index. So, if you took the monthly prices of a stock over a three-year period and plotted them on a graph you could see either how close together they are or how far apart they are. The further apart they are, the more volatile the stock is. How far they vary from the average price of the three years is called the variance"

8.3　Explain in your own words what "volatility" is?

8.4　Explain in your own words what "variance" is?

Beta, R-Squared, and Standard Deviation

"Take *Beta* for instance. No, it's not that old video tape you have in your closet and were hoping would be valuable one day. Beta is a measure of risk or volatility as it relates to an index. Let's say a mutual fund you own has a Beta of 1 to the S&P 500 Index. This fund would then tend to go up about the same as the S&P and down about the same. If the Beta was 1.5, the fund would be 50% more volatile than the S&P. If the Beta was .5 then the fund would be 50% less volatile than the S&P."

"*Alpha*, another well-used Wall Street term, is used to measure how much the fund's performance is better than the correlated benchmark index. If the fund's Alpha is 5, it outperformed its benchmark index by 5%."

"*Standard Deviation* is the "wobble factor", showing us how much a fund wobbles back and forth from its average return. The more it wobbles, the higher the risk.

Technically, Standard Deviation measures how a fund's performance over time is different from its average return. (2) The greater the difference, the higher the volatility. The higher the volatility, the more uncertainty in future returns."

> "When the daily standard deviations are increasing, there is generally more fear in the markets, and thus more potential risk. The most common manifestation of the measurements of the standard deviation in real time is called the "VIX". The "VIX" is a measurement of the implied volatility of how the options that are used to protect portfolios are being priced in real time by traders in the S&P 500 markets." *Navi Dowty, CFA*

"*R-Squared* is interesting because it is the assessor of measurements. This measurement grades the accuracy of the assets movements that can be related to a benchmark index. If the grade is low, 70 or less, the Beta is probably not reliable. If the grade is higher than 85, the Beta might be considered to be more dependable. R-Squared sheds light on the veracity of risk measurements." (3)

8.5 Explain in your own words the concept of "beta."

8.6 Explain in your own words the concept of "alpha."

8.7 Explain in your own words the concept of "standard deviation."

8.8 Explain in your own words the concept of "R-squared."

8.9 In what ways would these concepts be helpful in evaluating your assets?

Stock Type Risk vs. Bond Type Risk

"…the question for Column C Red Risk Money is this: what percent of your Red Risk Money do you want in stock-type risk and what percent do you want in bond-type risk? It is perfectly okay to have all of one and none of the other, or a simple 50% portion of each. It's up to your comfort level."

"I also have a rule for Red Risk Money that unless you have over two million dollars in investible assets, you probably want to stay away from individual stocks. I'm not talking about the stock your company gave you or stock inherited from your father. Individual stocks concentrate the risk on a single company rather than spreading the risk over many companies or markets. Unless you are very market savvy, you don't want in this game as a conservative investor."

"The reason I don't believe you want to get into individual stocks is simple: risk is concentrated into one stock or a bundle of maybe 30 to 50 stocks if you have a manager. I believe the better route for the conservative investor is to spread the risk around with mutual funds or Exchange Traded Funds (ETF's)."

"I also believe that, for the most part, owning individual bonds does the same thing to the bond-type risk that owning individual stocks does to the stock-type risk category. While using bond funds doesn't give you the potential to get your principal back at the end of the term, it can spread the bond risk around between many different bonds and types of bonds.

However, there is a significant disadvantage to bond funds. Since bonds can lose value in a rising interest rate climate, owning an individual bond that has an end at which time you can redeem your principal might be a good option for bond-type risk in Column C. The problem with individual bonds is the quality of the company issuing the bond. If you bought Enron or Bear Stearns bonds, you could have lost money. I actually think that a tactically managed account of bond funds is the best approach in bond-type risk for the conservative investor."

8.10 **Do you agree or disagree with the "two million dollar rule?" Explain.**

8.11 **What do you think about the author's viewpoint on bond-type risk?**

Who Chooses the Assets?

"I believe that finding a good Registered Investment Advisor who charges a fee for asset management might be the optimal choice here. The reason is if you don't know anything about mutual funds, whether they are stock or bond related, you will have a hard time maximizing the potential of this area. I'm a bottom-line type who believes paying a fee for a good service is better than losing money because I'm too cheap.

However, I believe brokers from large broker dealers represent the same old Wall Street mentality. They are very predictable in what they recommend. Usually some well-known family of funds like American Funds, T. Rowe Price, ING, Fidelity, or proprietary funds, are used along with a smattering of bonds and a variable annuity or two. It is a commission-driven model. Commissions paid on trading stocks or mutual funds are so low they are not a consideration anymore. The real money is made for brokers in the shares of mutual funds and commissions on variable annuities. These assets can provide both immediate and ongoing commissions."

"When choosing someone to manage your Red Risk Money, whether you choose a Registered Investment Advisor or a broker, it's important to find out how long they have been managing. You would also want to know their management "style;" what is the system they use to determine their investments, do they have a proven specialty, and what is their track record? Most importantly you want to know how they manage risk."

8.12 How would you go about choosing an asset manager?

Tactical vs. Buy & Hold Management

"There are two styles of management that you might choose from: tactical or "buy & hold." Simply put, tactical management is active, daily management. In a "buy & hold" style, the manager chooses the sectors of the market, how much to weight each sector and then uses the best fund managers available. So in essence, the advisor is trying to choose an all-star team of managers and let them do the buying and selling of assets inside the funds."

"Choosing an all-star team of fund managers can be great when the all-star is riding a winning streak. But when the streak ends, it can be ugly. For instance, in 2007 an all-star fund favorite was Ken Heebner and the CGM Focus fund, which returned 79.97% for the year. But in 2008, Heebner gave back -48.18% and then under-performed the market in 2009 with a 10.42% return.(4) Take a look at what that meant for you, the investor.

$1,000 in CGM Focus Fund (CGMFX):
01-10-2007 $1,000
12-31-2007 $1,800
12-31-2008 $933
12-31-2009 $1,030

(*Returns based on YahooFinance data)

For a conservative investor, the above numbers are just too volatile. Yes, you were ahead of the game by the end of 2009, but the road to get there was far too bumpy. Besides, if you were like the average investor who pulls out when the market is down, you would never have recovered your $1,000 in 2009, as you sat on the sidelines licking your wounds.

The vaunted American Funds Growth Fund of America, used by many commissioned based brokers, was not any better. (5)

$1,000 in American Funds Growth Fund of America (AGTHX):
01-10-2007 $1,000
12-31-2007 $1,110
12-31-2008 $676
12-31-2009 $909
*(*Returns based on YahooFinance data)*

Not only was the road bumpy, but you lost some luggage in the end. So, choosing an all-star team of fund managers and sitting on them while you pay fees or commissions can be frustrating. "Buy & hold" is definitely a more growth-oriented risk tolerance management style."

8.13   What do you think are the positives and negatives of the "buy & hold" management strategy?

"…a more tactical management style can yield some surprising results. The first plus for a tactical management style is its daily nature. Tactical managers seek to find returns by moving in and out of markets or segments of the market to take advantage of anomalies and strengths in certain market sectors depending on what they see in their analytical research and forecasts. They can be "all in" or "all out" on any given day.

Generally speaking, tactical managers choose a broad category such as equity growth and watch trends in that segment of the market to determine if they want to be in or out. At its best, it is done with a pre-determined process or model that dictates whether the manager buys, sells, or holds his position. A manager pulls the buy/sell trigger, but the process should determine the decision he makes, not his emotions.

Tactical management is the wave of the future because it is information driven and the investing world travels at the speed of the internet. It is a completely different world than it was even ten years ago and the future will probably be ruled by tactical managers."

"…Column C Red Money Investing is where the risk is in the ABC Model. You can choose stock-type risk or bond-type risk, and how much you want in either category."

Disclaimer: *Certain statements contained herein may be statements of future expectations and other forward-looking statements that are based on author's current views and assumptions and involve known and unknown risks and uncertainties that could cause actual results, performance or events to differ materially from those expressed or implied in such statements. In addition to statements which are forward-looking by reason of context, the words 'may, will, should, expects, plans, intends, anticipates, believes, estimates, predicts, potential, or continue' and similar expressions identify forward-looking statements.*

Actual results, performance or events may differ materially from those in such statements due to, without limitation, (i) actual research performance, (ii) management expense ratios, (iii) size of market opportunity, (iv) changing levels of competition, (v) changes in laws and regulations, (vi) changes in process technologies, (vii) the impact of acquisitions, including related integration issues, (viii) reorganization measures, (ix) general competitive factors on a local, regional, national and/or global basis (x) and, financial projections. Many of these factors may be more likely to occur, or more pronounced, as a result of terrorist activities and their consequences.

The matters discussed herein may also involve risks and uncertainties. The author assumes no obligation to update any forward-looking information contained herein, and assumes no liability for the accuracy of any of the information presented herein as of a future date.

Chapter Eight Notes

Chapter Nine

What if it Happened Again?
ABC's in a Bear Market

What if the worst bear market in history happened again?

"What would the worst bear market in history do to your portfolio, which carries with it your lifestyle in retirement?"

Most would argue the worst bear market started with the Crash of 1929 and didn't recover from its market high, until the fall of 1954 a 25-year bear."

"It is generally accepted that a bear market is a 20% drop in the broad market indexes such as the Dow Jones Industrial Average or the S&P 500 over a two month period. Bear markets are a time of deep pessimism, falling stock prices, and usually high volatility. A bear is not to be confused with a correction. The correction is usually a short period of time, something less than two months, while a bear market is two months or longer. (1)

There were two very large and very long bear markets in the twentieth century. As I previously mentioned the 1929 crash which lasted to 1954, and then the 1965-1982 bear market. Most seniors remember both and boomers definitely remember the gas lines of the 70's bear market. Russell Napier in his book *The Anatomy of a Bear* says on average every three years there's a bear market, every eight years there's a stinker of a bear market, and big bears last an average of 17 years. Napier also says the bear market that started in 2000 wouldn't end until 2011-2014, probably closer to the latter, with the Dow at less than 5000. (2)"

"The way to make money is to buy when blood is running in the streets." John D. Rockefeller" (3)

9.1   How do you interpret Rockefeller's statement?

"We simply attempt to be fearful when others are greedy and to be greedy only when others are fearful." Warren Buffett" (4)

9.2 **Following Warren Buffett's advice, when would you want to place money in the market?**

Using the ABC Model in a Bear Market

"...the ABC Model of Investing shines its brightest, because investing in the three categories will almost always increase opportunities for success in a long hard bear market. In fact, when others have lost money in a buy-and-hold mentality believing the market will recover over an extended period of time, those who have diversified in the ABC Model have made money.

Using the ten years of the market from 2000 through 2009 as an example, let's see how the ABC's would have performed. If Russell Napier and other economists are right, the current bear started with the tech-bubble bursting in 2000, this would be a good ten years to view." (5)

WHAT IF...? : S&P 500 LAST 10 YEARS

Investable Assets: $500,000

Current Asset Allocation

2000 - 2009 S&P 500 Returns:	Interest A 3%	Cap B 7%	C S&P 500	Total	Dollar Gain/Loss	Percent Gain/Loss
	$50,000	$0	$450,000	$500,000		
-10.14%	$51,500	$0	$404,370	$455,870	-$44,130	-9%
-13.04%	$53,045	$0	$351,640	$404,685	-$51,185	-11%
-23.37%	$54,636	$0	$269,462	$324,098	-$80,587	-20%
26.38%		-$101,786		$396,821	$72,723	23%
8.99%				$429,125	$32,303	8%
3.00%	$59,703	$0	$382,296	$441,998	$12,874	4%
13.62%	$61,494	$0	$434,464	$495,858	$53,860	12%
3.53%	$63,339	$0	$449,698	$513,036	$17,178	3%
-38.49%	$65,239	$0	$276,609	$341,848	-$171,188	-34%
19.67%	$67,196	$0	$331,018	$398,214	$56,366	16%
Total After 10 Yrs:	$67,196	$0	$331,018	$398,214	-$101,786	-20%
Current %:	10%	$0	90%			

"The illustration above shows the S&P 500 returns (6) for the years 2000 through 2009 on the left. The investible assets are $500,000. This example shows a typical investor who has about 10% in cash earning an average of 3% and 90% allocated to the market represented by the S&P 500. We use the broad market index to approximate what investing in the market in general was like over that period of time. Certainly an investor could have been in more or less risk than illustrated here. Yet, the illustration shows in general terms how the market performed from 2000-2009. Notice, there are no monies allocated to Column B, which are Index Annuities.

The chart shows at the end of the ten-year period, this investor would have lost over $100,000. I don't know about you, but a 20% loss in the market is devastating when it comes to retirement!* Imagine if you were 52 years old in 2000 and planning to retire when most people retire at age 62. Would you do what many have had to do, which is work another 3-5 years in hopes of recovering those assets needed to retire?"

9.3 What if the next ten years saw a 20% loss in the market, how would it affect your retirement?

"And what if it happens again? What if the next ten years aren't any better than the last ten years? Can you afford to lose another 20% or possibly more? Can you continue to push off your retirement indefinitely?

Most people don't realize there could be an alternative to losing money over a decade long Bear market. Take a look at the graph below and judge for yourself.

WHAT IF...? : S&P 500 LAST 10 YEARS

Current Asset Allocation

2000 - 2009 S&P 500 Returns:	Interest A 3% $50,000	Cap B 7% $300,000	C S&P 500 $150,000	Total $500,000	Dollar Gain/Loss	Percent Gain/Loss
-10.14%	$51,500	$300,000	$134,790	$486,290	-$13,710	-3%
-13.04%	$53,045	$300,000	$117,213	$470,258	-$16,032	-3%
-23.37%	$54,636	$300,000	$89,821	$444,457	-$25,801	-5%
26.38%	$56,275	$321,000	$113,515	$490,791	$46,334	10%
8.99%		$198,655 Difference		$525,154	$34,363	7%
3.00%				$540,909	$15,755	3%
13.62%				$584,820	$43,911	8%
3.53%	$63,339	$391,901	$149,899	$605,138	$20,318	3%
-38.49%	$65,239	$391,901	$92,203	$549,342	-$55,796	-9%
19.67%	$67,196	$419,334	$110,339	$596,869	$47,427	9%
Total After 10 Yrs:	$67,196	$419,334	$110,339	$596,869	$96,869	19%
Desired %:	10%	60%	30%			

79

"Using the same $500,000 over the identical ten years (7), let's allocate 60% to short-term laddered maturities in indexed annuities. Assuming an average index cap of 7% we begin to see how the ABC Model is a great model to use for bear markets. This time period was a bear market and yet the allocation made $96,869 over the same time period while the first example lost $101,786. That's a difference of $198,655 over a really nasty decade."

Why the ABC Model Works

"The first rule is not to lose. The second rule is not to forget the first rule." <u>Warren Buffett</u> *(8)*

"Mr. Buffet helps us to understand why the ABC Model works so well. The key is simply to protect your principal and retain your gains. Remember Green Money Rules #1 and #2? That's right. Green Money Rule #1 is the same as the first rule for Warren Buffet. Don't lose! Look at the Red Column C in the years 2000 through 2002. You started with $150,000 in 2000 and ended with $89,000. Remember the "Tech-Bubble?" If you were invested in tech-stocks in those years you took a much greater beating. Now look at the same years in the Green Column B. You started with $300,000 and ended with $300,000. Are you happy? Darn right! You didn't gain anything, but you didn't LOSE anything. Zero is your Hero!

Look down the Red Money Column at the ninth year, 2008, and the loss of 38%. It took you five years to just about get back to where you started in 2000 and then the bottom dropped out. You lost $55,796 and only had $92,203 left of your Red Risk money. Yet, peer into the ninth year of the Green Money Column and notice you didn't lose a dime and have $391,901* which is more money than you started with in the year 2000."

"…you can diversify with Fixed Principal Assets like laddered maturities of Fixed Indexed Annuities and the decade wouldn't have been the abysmal lost decade of 2000 through 2009."

9.4 **Do you see the market over the next decade more or less volatile than the previous ten years? Explain.**

9.5 **Considering the ABC Model's performance in a Bear Market, is it something that you would use in your portfolio? Explain.**

"The decade from 2010 and forward doesn't look any better either. With government bailouts, increasing mortgage defaults, escalating taxes, a new government controlled health care system, and a fifteen trillion dollar rising deficit, something is going to get ugly."

Disclaimer: *This information is not intended to give tax, legal, or investment advice. Please seek advice from a qualified professional on these matters. Past performance is no guarantee future results. Example uses a 7% cap and assumes no dollars withdrawn from accounts. Crediting rates including caps for FIA's can change and are determined by the insurance companies at the time of issue, Annuity Contracts are products of the insurance industry and are not guaranteed by any bank or insured by the FDIC. When purchasing a fixed indexed annuity, you own an annuity contract backed by the insurance company, you are not purchasing shares of stocks or indexes. Product features such as interest rates, caps, and participation rates may vary by product and state and may be subject to change. Surrender charges may apply for early withdrawals. Be sure to review the specific product disclosure for more details. Guarantees are based on the financial strength and claims paying ability of the insurance company. Lifetime income benefit riders are used to calculate lifetime payments only. The income account value is not available for cash surrender or in a death benefit. Excess withdrawals may reduce lifetime income and may incur surrender charges. Fees may apply. Guarantees based on the financial strength and claims paying ability of the insurance company. See specific product disclosure for more details.*

Chapter Nine Notes

FINANCIAL ABC's
of retirement planning

Chapter Ten

The Cowboy Preacher
The Biggest Need for Retirees:
Income Planning

"The concept of retirement in America grew out of the reforms made in the great depression; the most significant of course was Social Security. In 1933, Congress passed the Social Security bill that enabled people who were age 65 to receive income checks monthly from the government starting in 1935. It was originally intended as a supplement to income for the elderly, yet has turned into the major source of income for many retirees. It is interesting to note the average retirement age in 1910 was 74 years old, and the average in 2006 was age 62." (1)

10.1   Why do you think the average retirement age is 62?

10.2   When do you plan to retire? Why then?

"It's interesting to note according to government actuarial tables a male age 62 is expected to live to just about 80 years old. If he reaches 75 he's expected to reach age 85, and if he reaches age 85 he's expected to live until age 90 plus. Women of those ages (never ask though) are expected to live another year and a half to two years longer than their male counter parts." (2)

"Still, life happens. And as I said, it happens for three decades on average in retirement. The highs and lows. The arthritis and dementia. The grandkids and poodles. Three decades of life all of which we have to fund. While there is so much more to enjoying retirement than money, if you screw up the money it has a dramatic impact on all the other aspects of those Golden Years. In fact, if you screw the money up you may have to go to work at the Golden Arches!"

"Inflation relates to how effective your buying power will remain for the course of your retirement. Even with straight-line inflation figured at 3%, what costs a $1 today will cost $2.40 when the 62-year-old couple's last survivor reaches 90.

And what, may I ask, inflates at only 3% for retirees?"

"What is the answer? Is risking principal in the stock market to chase 10%–12 % gains the answer? Certainly, in the past the market has been the place to beat inflation. In 1950 the S&P 500 ranged from 17 to 23. In 2010 the S&P fluctuated between 1,000 and 1,200. (3) Yes, more than 50 times what it was 60 years prior. That is fantastic considering we have had 13 bear markets in those 60 years…some dipping thirty percent or more!! So, on the surface at least, the risk is worth the reward.

What happens if the next 60 years doesn't play out like the last 60 years? Or the next 30 years like the last 30 years, or for that matter the next 10 years? Do you have 60 years to overcome losses?"

10.3   How would you plan for three decades of income?

10.4   How would your income plan account for the threat of market losses?

Accumulation vs. Distribution

"Retirement happens in thirds. Let me explain. Remember, with life expectancies for couples in retirement lasting 20 to 30 years you have to fund retirement for three decades to be safe. We are living longer and it ain't gettin' cheaper! This makes it incredibly important to know the difference between investing for accumulation and investing for distribution…"

To Illustrate, I have created a hypothetical 10-year market index. If you started in the first year with $500,000 and put that money in the sample index, at the end of 10 years you would have $631,205, assuming no withdrawals.

Let me ask you a question though. If you inverted the index over the same 10-year period of time, so the 10th year return would flip to be the first year return, the 9th year would be the second year return and so on would the final dollar amount be the same? Now, most people (including me) when first asked this question intuitively say "no." You would have to have a different number, right?

Wrong. The commutative principal of multiplication states that when multiplying numbers, you can put them in any order and the result will be the same (see illustration below).

Hypothetical Index
Beginning Value $500,000

Year	Annual Return	End of Year Value	Inverse Return	End of Year Value
1	28%	$640,000	-38%	$310,000
2	-10%	$576,000	-12%	$272,800
3	15%	$662,400	2%	$278,256
4	17%	$775,008	15%	$319,994
5	1%	$782,758	26%	$403,193
6	26%	$986,275	1%	$407,225
7	15%	$1,134,216	17%	$479,453
8	2%	$1,156,901	15%	$547,921
9	-12%	$1,018,073	-10%	$493,129
10	-38%	**$631,205**	28%	**$631,205**

That's right! You can put all the negative numbers at the beginning, middle, end, or scatter them throughout the years and you will end up with the same number each time! That is unless you take money out of the equation."

10.5 Have losses to your portfolio ever changed your plans for retirement? Explain.

"Let's say you start again in the first year with the same $500,000, use the same 10-year hypothetical index returns, yet this time take out an income stream for retirement. Let's take out $35,000 a year and use a 3% rate of inflation. So, each year we would see the withdrawal grow to cover rising expenses until in the 10th year the withdrawal is $45,667. If we use the same index returns we end up with $313,017. Not bad! It seems to really work.

Hypothetical Index
Beginning Value $500,000   Withdrawal $35,000   Inflation 3%

Year	Annual Return	Annual Withdrawal	End of Year Value
1	28%	$35,000	$605,000
2	-10%	$36,050	$508,450
3	15%	$37,132	$547,586
4	17%	$38,245	$602,430
5	1%	$39,393	$569,062
6	26%	$40,575	$676,443
7	15%	$41,792	$736,118
8	2%	$43,046	$707,795
9	-12%	$44,337	$578,522
10	-38%	**$45,667**	**$313,017**

However, if we invert the returns again, so year 10 is now year one and so on, we run out of money in year eleven! That's incredible isn't it? One way it works for 10 years, but simply invert the numbers as below, and you run out of money in ten years. If you are retired, you are headed back to work!

Hypothetical Index
Beginning Value $500,000   Withdrawal $35,000   Inflation 3%

Year	Annual Return	Annual Withdrawal	End of Year Value
1	-38%	$35,000	$275,000
2	-12%	$36,050	$205,950
3	2%	$37,132	$172,938
4	15%	$38,245	$160,633
5	26%	$39,393	$163,004
6	1%	$40,575	$124,060
7	17%	$41,792	$103,358
8	15%	$43,046	$75,816
9	-10%	$44,337	$23,898
10	28%	**$45,667**	**-$15,078**

Why does this happen? It's simple. The biggest losing year was the first year, followed by another losing year. In the first example, the first year was positive followed by a smaller loss.

You see the problem is we can't know when the losses will happen and how significant they will be. If it is true that we have to plan for three decades of retirement, not knowing when the losses will happen, means we have to plan very carefully."

10.6 How might an ABC model help with your plans in retirement? Explain.

"That's why the ABC Model is a logical alternative to Wall Street for the most conservative of investors. You can preserve principal, retain your gains, and even guarantee income.

There are many ways to guarantee income. Yet, guaranteeing income, principal, and gains at the same time is the magic of Fixed Indexed Annuities with Guaranteed Income Benefits, along with a well thought out strategy for each third of retirement."

Green Money Income Plans

"The standard Wall Street model is to mix bonds and stocks in a portfolio and take an annual percentage out of the account, say 4% to 6%, for income and see if the account will last a lifetime. In other words, they hope the return is high enough to make the income last and they pray the inevitable bear market losses won't destroy their retirement dream. I tell clients, instead of hoping and praying an income plan will work, let's just guarantee it."

"One of the income plans that fit into the ABC Model is a concept called, "Split Annuity Income." This is the practice of creating income by putting part of the assets designated to create income into an immediate annuity, one that pays a monthly income right away and ending after a specified number of years. The left over part of the assets designated to create income is placed in a deferred annuity for growth which will be used to create an increase in income when the immediate annuity ends. Take a look at the following Split Annuity Illustration #1.

Split Annuity Illustration #1: Ten Year Split*
Beginning Value
$500,000

10 Year Income Bucket
Allotment: $215,000
Annual: $25,271
Monthly: $2,106
Annual Taxable Amount: $5,054
Value After 10 Years: $0

Growth Bucket
Allotment: $285,000
Bonus: 8%
LIBR: 6.5%
Years Deferred: 10

Beginning of 11th Year
Guaranteed Income Account Value (not cash): $577,783

11th Year Income by Guaranteed Withdrawals
- Ages 60 to 69 at 5%: $28,889
- Ages 70 to 79 at 6%: $34,667
- Ages 80 and up at 7%: $40,445

Illustration #1 shows the concept of a Ten-Year Split Annuity. In this illustration, we assume an example of $500,000 of investible assets allocated to create income in retirement. The left side of the illustration uses less than half the total amount designated for the plan, $215,000, in an immediate annuity for 10 years. It creates an income of $25,271 a year or $2,106 month. If the $215,000 is coming from after-tax monies, the tax benefits on the income are significant. Of the $25,271 a year of income, roughly $5,054 is taxable during the first ten years. *(All rates are assumed and income is estimated not actual. Actual rates will be those used at the time of annuitization with the specific insurance company chosen. The illustration is an estimate based on current annuitization tables.)"*

"Second, on the right side of the illustration we place the balance of the original amount, $285,000, in a Fixed Indexed Annuity offering an 8% bonus, and a Lifetime Income Benefit Rider (LIBR) of 6.5%. We let it grow for ten years, while the first annuity finishes paying out. The income rider increases the premium by the 8% bonus, and then calculates growth for income purposes by 6.5% each year. This is not cash growth, only a calculated benefit to determine income in the future. If the person owning this income plan is 65 to start with, his immediate income side will run out in ten years, depleting principal and interest over those ten years. Yet, the second half has a guaranteed income of $34,667 at age 75, an increase of over $9,000 a year of income.

The cash account created in the second bucket is still growing according to the index returns of the annuity, and is depleted as the income payments are taken out. It doesn't matter if the cash is depleted by low index returns and income leaving the account because the income is guaranteed for the rest of your life, no matter what happens to the cash value of the contract."

"You could use the Ten Year Split Annuity as illustrated above or a Five Year Split Annuity (Illustration 2) which allows for more diversity in the plan giving the retiree a chance to change the plan in five years rather than ten years. In the Five-Year Split you only use $122,620 in the immediate annuity that pays the same $25,271 a year, but for five years instead of ten. Using the balance of $377,380 in another annuity with an 8% bonus creates a guaranteed income of $33,504 at age 70, over an $8,000 a year increase. Remember the $33,504 is guaranteed for the rest of your life, no matter what happens to the cash in the account due to any lean years in the market where the index credits would be low."

Split Annuity Illustration #2: Five Year Split*
Beginning Value
$500,000

5 Year Income Bucket
Allotment: $122,620
Annual: $25,271
Monthly: $2,106
Annual Taxable Amount: $4,549
Value After 5 Years: $0

Growth Bucket
Allotment: $377,380
Bonus: 8%
LIBR: 6.5%
Years Deferred: 5

Beginning of 6th Year
Guaranteed Income Account Value (not cash): $558,407

11th Year Income by Guaranteed Withdrawals
- Ages 60 to 69 at 5%: $27,920
- Ages 70 to 79 at 6%: $33,504
- Ages 80 and up at 7%: $39,088

"Guaranteeing income using ABC-Model strategies creates some freedom in retirement lifestyles—freedom and security. Like I said, if you screw up the first third of retirement, it affects so many other facets that make a fulfilling retirement. Hoping and praying the market won't take a downturn and swallow your money whole along with your dreams of the "Golden Years" is not a solution. Green Money Guarantees are the solution."

10.7 Is guaranteeing income important to you in retirement? Explain?

10.8 What do you like most about the Split Annuity concepts?

10.9 What do you like least about them?

__Disclaimer:__ This information is not intended to give tax, legal, or investment advice. Please seek advice from a qualified professional on these matters. Annuity Contracts are products of the insurance industry and are not guaranteed by any bank or insured by the FDIC. When purchasing a fixed indexed annuity, you own an annuity contract backed by the insurance company, you are not purchasing shares of stocks or indexes. Product features such as interest rates, caps, and participation rates may vary by product and state and may be subject to change. Surrender charges may apply for early withdrawals. Be sure to review the specific product disclosure for more details. Guarantees are based on the financial strength and claims paying ability of the insurance company.

Lifetime income benefit riders are used to calculate lifetime payments only. The income account value is not available for cash surrender or in a death benefit. Excess withdrawals may reduce lifetime income and may incur surrender charges. Fees may apply. Guarantees based on the financial strength and claims paying ability of the insurance company. See specific product disclosure for more details.

Chapter Ten Notes

FINANCIAL ABC's
of retirement planning

Chapter Eleven

I Should Have Listened
Seven Problems with Your 401(k)

401(k) Plan: Remodel or Replace

"Don't get me wrong. I'm not going to suggest that your 401(k) is in need of repair. It is what it is and you can't do a thing about it until you get out of it. Actually, it's not just in need of repair or remodeling. If you are in retirement or close to it, you will probably want to replace it. A 401(k) plan is a great place to be while you're employed, but once you retire or maybe a little before, it's time to get out."

"In 1978, the US Internal Revenue Code was remodeled to add section 401(k), which allowed employees to defer a part of their income into personal savings accounts. Monies deposited in the account are not included as income in the year they were deducted and not taxed until income is taken out. By 2003, 438,000 companies had developed 401(k) plans and by 2007, Americans had $3 trillion dollars invested in 401(k) plans." *(1)(2)*

"While you are still working, and especially if your employer is matching your deposits or part of your deposits, a 401(k) plan is a great place to be. Once you retire, though, there are some better options. There are even pre-retirement options available. Let's take a look at seven possible problems with 401(k) plans and why you should do a little remodeling of your retirement assets."

Seven Problems with Your 401(k)

Problem #1: Is Your 401k Compliant?

"Is your employer or former employer's 401k plan compliant? Will it stay compliant throughout your retirement years? You would think this is an "automatic yes," but apparently not. The IRS on its website has some enlightening information as it relates to plans that go bad.

It appears that beginning in 2002, the IRS started to examine Form 5500 returns for 401(k) plans in various geographical areas throughout the country. They analyzed these returns and identified issues in detail.

> "The issues identified in the examination of 401(k) plans within the various market segments mirrored those identified in 401(k) plans as a whole. The cause

of these errors varied from case-to-case. However, the overwhelming identified cause of an error occurring in 401(k) plans within the completed market segments was the Failure to Follow the Terms of the Plan." (3)

The rather astounding discovery of the IRS analysis was that the employer failed to follow the rules of its own plan documents. The IRS even lists the top ten reasons for plan failure right on their website.(4) Of course we all know that trying to follow the IRS and its details is akin to nailing Jell-O to a wall, but these are professionals who make the mistakes, not amateurs."

"The question is how do you know your company is following the rules? Do you simply trust your company as most do? It would seem important for a successful retirement that your assets reside in a secure environment where they are free from the kind of exposure listed on the IRS Website. The reason is simple: failure of a 401(k) plan triggers total taxation of plan benefits for everyone in the plan!

Granted, this doesn't happen often because the IRS will allow the sponsoring company a certain amount of leeway to make corrections. Yet, I can't help thinking of all the broken pension promises over the years from highly reputable companies who cut benefits for retirees because they messed up the pension fund. It's just a thought. Maybe pulling money out of your 401(k) and taking control of it before somebody at the home office screws up the accounting might make sense."

11.1   Is it possible your 401(k) plan is at risk by IRS standards?

Problem #2: Roth accounts in a 401(k) have issues

"A Roth opened inside a 401(k) account is referred to as a DRAC, a **D**esignated **R**etirement **A**ccount, and has to follow a different set of rules than a normal Roth IRA."

"Monies deposited in a Roth IRA are tax-free once the account has passed it's "non-exclusion" period of 5 years. Money can be withdrawn prior to the five years on a FIFO (First In, First Out) basis, which simply means your principal is taken out first. Yet after the 5-year period, all monies withdrawn are tax free." (5)

"The IRS also considers the Roth beginning date for any Roth contributions as January 1st of the year in which the account was opened. For example, if you opened a Roth on November 15th of 2010, the start date of the "non-exclusion" period would be January 1st of 2010. The client could then start taking tax-free withdrawals from the account January 1st, 2015. Opening a contributory Roth account begins the 5-year "non-exclusion" period for all ensuing Roth accounts, unless they're in a 401(k). If a Roth is a DRAC, then each new Roth opened inside other 401(k) plans with subsequent employers start a new 5-year period before tax-free money can be withdrawn.(6)

A Roth account inside a 401(k) plan is also subject to the same rules as the 401(k) plan. There is one rule that is especially troublesome for a Roth inside a 401(k). A Roth inside a 401(k) is subject to the Required Minimum Distribution rules. In other words, you would be required to start taking income out of your Roth at age 70 and a half just like a regular IRA.(7) This is not true with a Roth outside a 401(k) plan.

The lifetime RMD rules can only be prevented by rolling the DRAC to a Roth IRA outside the 401(k) plan.

The DRAC 5-year non-exclusion period does not carry over to the new Roth IRA. Opening a Roth account, outside a DRAC will begin the 5 year "non-exclusion" period for all ensuing contributory Roth accounts opened at later dates, as Natalie Choate says in her book, *Life and Death Planning for Retirement Benefits*:"

> *"The Five-Year Period (called in the statute the "nonexclusion period") for all of a participant's Roth IRAs begins on January 1 of the first year for which a contribution was made to any Roth IRA maintained for that participant."* (8)

"In other words, if a client opened a Roth on November 11th, 2010, the beginning date for figuring in the 5-year non-exclusion period for all other Roth accounts started after 2010 would then become January 1st, 2010." (9)

11.2 **Do you have a DRAC? If so, what would be the benefits of rolling it over to a Roth IRA outside of your 401(k) plan?**

Problem #3: Limited choices.

"Surely one of the greatest problems with 401(k) plans are the limited investment choices, especially when it comes to conservative investing. While larger company plans offer a variety of mutual fund companies and a few money markets they pale in comparison to the universe of options available outside a 401(k). Smaller companies have even fewer choices, some with only one family of funds.

This is a conservative investor's nightmare when it comes to finding an asset that doesn't experience market losses. Remember Warren Buffet's first rule of investing? Don't lose any money! Rule number two? Never forget rule number one."

11.3 **Does your plan have the choices you wish it had?**

11.4 **What choices would you like to add to your 401(k)?**

11.5 Are you confident in choosing between assets in your 401(k)?

"If having no protected accounts wasn't bad enough, all you have to help you decide where to invest is a little booklet explaining the options. It lists the fund families, shows the returns of all the mutual funds, and explains the rules. You look around for help, and the Human Resource personnel are nice people, but they are not financial advisors. The broker may come to the offices once a year. Some companies are located in a different city than the broker who set up the plan and employees have no access to him.

Of course, the final insult is the limited ability to make changes within your plan. To do so you either have to go online, run through the website maze, or call a toll free number and fumble through the company's phone options. If by chance you finally land on the right option, you end up misplacing your PIN number and have to start all over again!"

11.6 What has been your experience in trying to make changes within your plan?

Problem #4: The 20% Withholding Trap.

"You finally decide you want to get out of your 401(k) plan only to find out your company withheld 20% of your account, which you will have to pay the taxes on next year's return."

"First you have to understand what a "distributive rollover" is. You have probably heard you can receive money from a pre-tax dollar plan, put the money in your account and have 60 days to find a new plan and deposit the assets. That is called a distributive rollover because they distributed the money to you. However, with 401(k) plans the IRS rules require the plan to withhold (for federal tax) 20%. NO EXCEPTIONS! Since you don't receive the 20%, it is taxed at the end of the year as a distribution. Not only that, but you can only rollover once every 12 months."

"…how to avoid the 20% trap. Don't have the company make the check out to you, but rather have the plan make the check out to the company you want to invest with. Make use of what's called a "Trustee-to-Trustee Transfer." You never see the check; it is sent directly to the next company. No withholding.

In some instances, a plan will make the check out to the new company, but send it to you. Don't worry, this won't trigger any withholding. Simply forward the check on to the company you want to invest with."

11.7 **In what ways would knowing how to avoid the 20% tax trap help you in planning your retirement?**

Problem #5: Limited Beneficiary Options

"Don't take this wrong, but if your spouse is the only option listed on your 401(k), it's a bad thing. This is one of the more distressing items on the list. Most people would like the money in their plan to go to their spouse, but what happens if you and your spouse die in a tragic remodeling accident? (It could happen). Where does the money go? I'm sure the state you live in has planned for this, but I'm pretty confident you would not want the state to control this decision. The problem is many plans only have one place for a beneficiary or the participant never filled out a beneficiary form.

11.8 **When was the last time you checked the beneficiary designations on your qualified plans?**

"To solve this problem, check your beneficiary designations on your plan to make sure you have listed at least one person to receive your money—other than the state of course. You would be surprised at how many people have missed this step completely and die with no beneficiaries listed.

I would suggest you conduct a beneficiary review with a financial professional or legal counsel. They can run through your beneficiary options with you. It's important to not only list a primary beneficiary, but also "contingent" and "tertiary" beneficiaries. A primary beneficiary receives all the Plan assets when you pass away. If you and your primary beneficiary pass away together in a car accident (sorry), your listed "contingent" beneficiary or beneficiaries would inherit plan assets. Generally, you list your spouse as a primary beneficiary, followed by your children. You might have one primary and three contingent beneficiaries. The most common way to list contingent beneficiaries are by percentages. Just remember that the percentages have to add up to 100%.

You can also list "tertiary" beneficiaries, which are people who receive plan assets if you and your contingent beneficiaries die in a plane crash on your way to a family vacation, (again, sorry). That would mean you and your immediate family was most likely taken out of the inheritance picture. Then, you might want to list grandchildren, nieces, nephews, brothers, sisters, or parents.

Tertiary beneficiaries can be used in many ways to pass on assets in complex estate plans to help with taxation. If you don't think of it ahead of time, your children won't have helpful options come tax time. For instance, if one of your children wanted to "disclaim" their share of the inheritance and let their kids, your grandchildren, inherit the plan assets so they could avoid a heavy tax, you would have to plan out the option in advance.

Think of it this way. Primary beneficiaries are first level inheritors; contingent beneficiaries are second level inheritors; and tertiary beneficiaries are third level inheritors."

A common beneficiary designation people use is "equal shares," which means the plan assets are divided equally among the listed beneficiaries. You will also want to designate your beneficiaries as "per stirpes" or "per capita." If you don't, most plans usually default to "per capita." Huh? Sounds like a disease? It isn't. "Per stirpes" is a legal phrase meaning "by the roots" (Latin) or by the blood lines. "per capita" is another legal (Latin) term meaning "by the head."

So, let's use an "equal shares, per stirpes" distribution with an immediate family of four: father, mother, son & daughter. Also, the son has two children; a son and a daughter. The daughter has a daughter, too. The father and mother own assets jointly, as is usual. The father passes away first, leaving the family assets to his wife. Some years later the wife passes away in a car accident with the daughter. The son is then the only living member of the immediate family, and passes away at a ripe old age. How do the assets pass on to heirs?

Per Stirpes Distribution Illustration

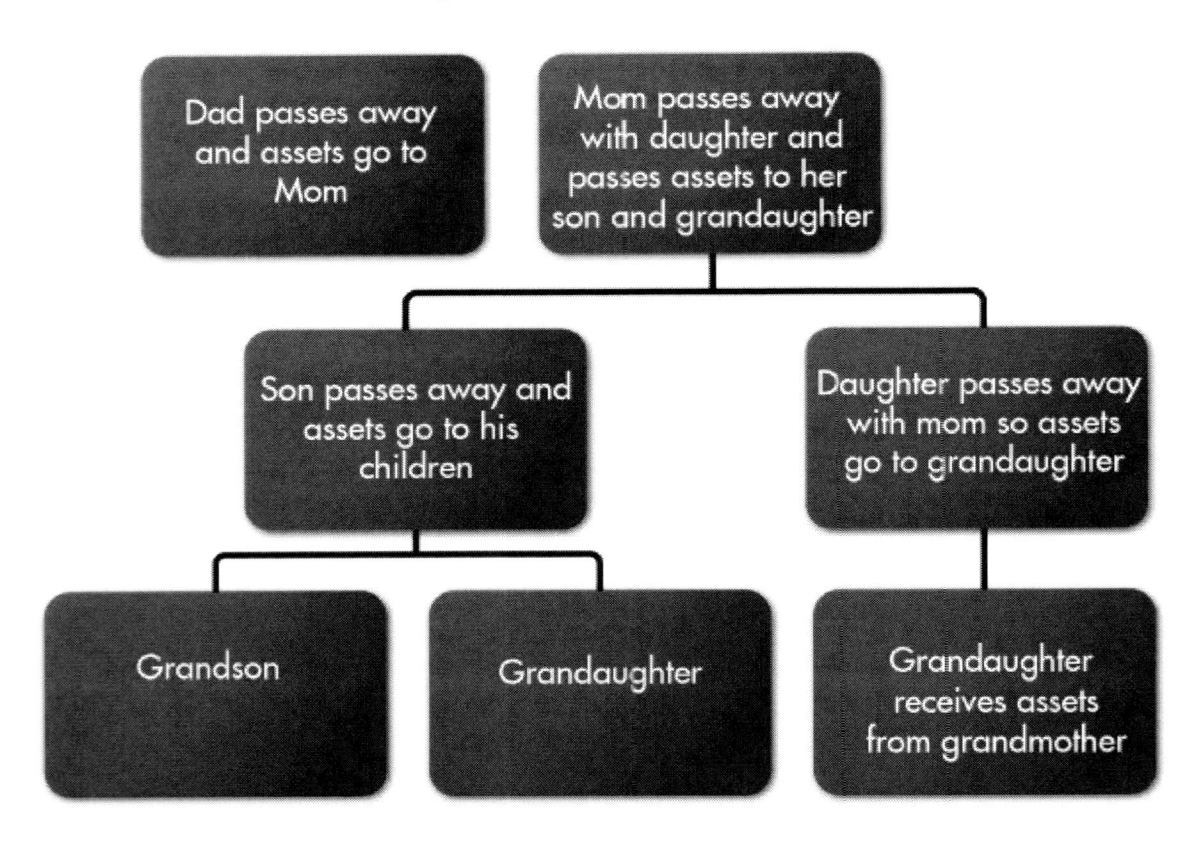

- Dad passes away and assets go to Mom
- Mom passes away with daughter and passes assets to her son and grandaughter
  - Son passes away and assets go to his children
    - Grandson
    - Grandaughter
  - Daughter passes away with mom so assets go to grandaughter
    - Grandaughter receives assets from grandmother

Per Capita Distribution Illustration

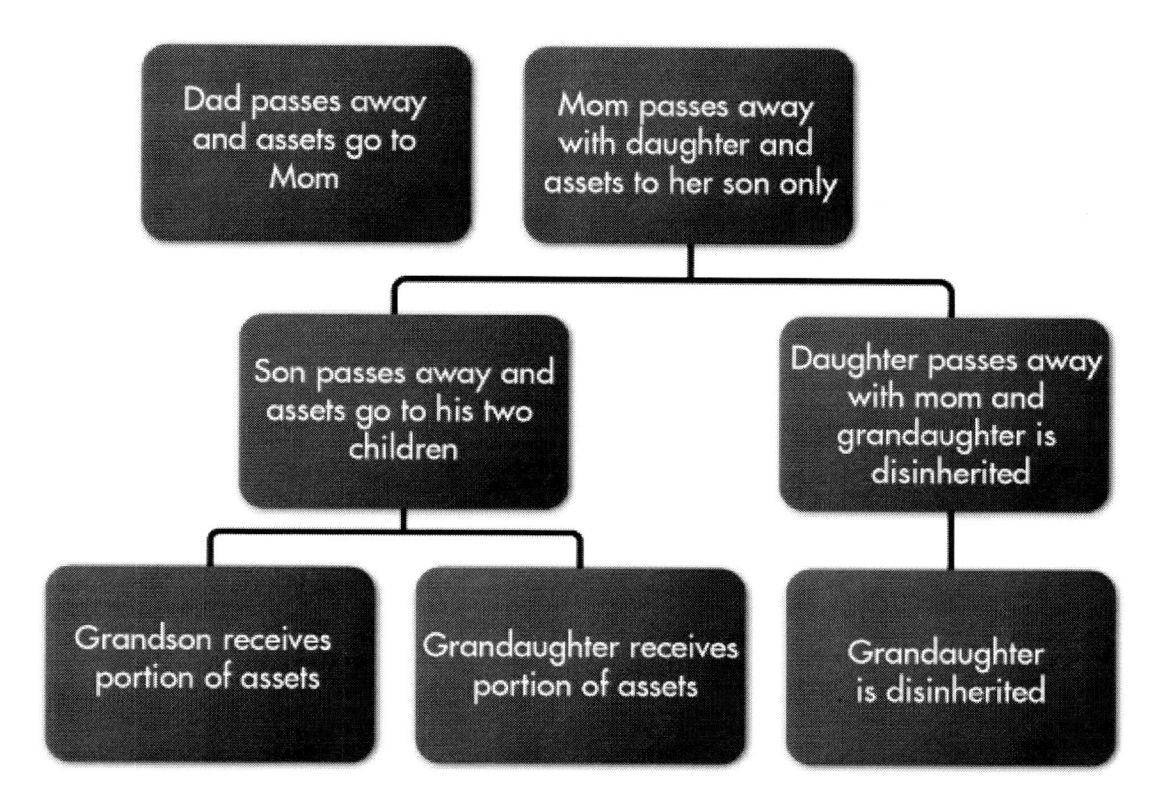

- Dad passes away and assets go to Mom
- Mom passes away with daughter and assets to her son only
  - Son passes away and assets go to his two children
    - Grandson receives portion of assets
    - Grandaughter receives portion of assets
  - Daughter passes away with mom and grandaughter is disinherited
    - Grandaughter is disinherited

If you listed "equal shares, per capita" under the same scenario described above, the family's assets would immediately pass to the son at the mother's death, disinheriting one of the grandchildren, the daughter's daughter.

> "You can see that a "beneficiary review" of your plan might be in order. One of the details you may discover about your 401(k) plan is that it doesn't provide for the any of the above listed options. That would simply be another reason to rollover your plan into an IRA where you can have exactly what you want to happen upon your demise a certainty."

11.9 Do you have any special family situations which need to be addressed with your beneficiary designations? Explain.

11.10 How would you arrange your beneficiaries?

Problem #6: Required Minimum Distribution Errors

11.11 **If you had a 401(k), and an IRA could you take a required minimum distribution out of one of them to cover the amount needed for both plans?**

"Many people along with many advisors make the same mistake of saying "yes." That's correct. "Yes" is a wrong answer. You must take a Required Minimum Distribution from each type of plan. A 401(k) RMD cannot cover other qualified plan RMD requirements. This may well be the most common mistake made amongst plan holders.

Yet, if you were to hold three separate IRA's, you could take one Required Minimum Distribution from just one of the accounts sufficient to cover all three accounts. This would allow you to take a distribution from an underperforming asset leaving more money in better performing assets. Imagine that kind of flexibility and you can imagine yourself out of your 401(k) plan, and into stronger options."

Problem #7: 401(k)'s are the Non-Stretch Plan

"A Stretch or Multi-Generational IRA plan is a plan in which your assets are passed to beneficiaries who leave them in the plan and simply take Required Minimum Distributions based on their IRS life expectancy tables. This allows the assets to grow tax-deferred over generations. Many 401(k) plans don't allow for this advantageous strategy."

"How a Stretch IRA Works*

Example: Papa John is 70 years old and is married to Jane, who is 66 years old. They have a 35-year-old daughter Jamie. John, the father, has accumulated $300,000 in his IRA. He begins his required minimum distributions when he reaches age 70 ½ based on his life expectancy of 13 years.

Beginning balance:	$300,000
Total RMD's before taxes:	$199,081
Total RMD's after taxes:	$143,338
Years of RMD payments:	13

Jane, his spouse, is his sole beneficiary. She inherits John's IRA when she is 79. She rolls the IRA balance into her own IRA. Jane names her daughter Jamie as the sole beneficiary. Jane takes her Required Minimum Distributions on her life expectancy of approximately 10 years.

IRA Jane inherited from John:	$326,331
Jane's total RMD's before taxes:	$205,864
Jane's total RMD's after taxes:	$148,222
Jane's total years of RMD's:	10

Jamie inherits her mother's IRA when she is 58. Instead of cashing out, she begins Required Minimum Distributions based on her life expectancy of approximately 25 years. Jamie designates her son, Jimmy, as her sole beneficiary.

IRA Jamie inherited from Jane:	$285,399
Jamie's total RMD's before taxes:	$537,137
Jamie's total RMD's after taxes:	$386,738
Jamie's total years of RMD's:	10

Jimmy inherits his mother Jamie's IRA and decides to cash it in to pay off his debts.

IRA Jimmy inherited from Jamie:	$121,128
Jimmy's total before taxes:	$121,128
Jimmy's total after taxes:	$87,212

Over three generations, John's $300,000 IRA paid his family over $1,063,209 before taxes! Unless this kind of opportunity for your family isn't important to you, you might want to make sure your retirement account is at a place where a Stretch IRA is possible. If not, your family might just say, "He should have listened!"

Note: This illustration assumes a 6% average annual total return and does not represent the performance of any specific investment. There is no guarantee of a 6% average annual return. The differences between actual and hypothetical results can result in significant differences between this illustration and the actual required distributions. The examples don't take into consideration estate taxes, but assumes a federal income tax rate of 28%. RMD's are calculated using life expectancy factors from the Uniform Lifetime Table for IRA owners and Single Life Expectancy Table for non-spouse beneficiaries (IRS Publication 590)."

11.12 How could a stretch IRA benefit your family situation?

Understanding Your 401(k) Options

"Once you understand that your 401(k) plan may not be the best place to leave retirement money, it's important to know your options. First, you can stay put and enjoy the same portfolio of funds that you may have liked, the same tax-deferred growth, and litigation protection for up to a million dollars."

"Many Plans have what is called an "In-Service, Non-Hardship Distribution" clause which allows you the availability of some, if not all, of your plan funds prior to retirement, post age 59 and a half. The IRS allows you to rollover your plan assets into a qualified IRA plan without taxation or a penalty so there is no reason for your employer's plan not to allow it. It is usually an oversight, if anything.

> *"Employers and 401(k) plan administrators don't advertise this fact, but most workers 59 and a half and older, and even some younger ones, **can roll over 401(k) funds while they're still working…70% of companies--and 89% of those with 5,000 or more employees--allow these in-service withdrawals**, the Profit Sharing/401k Council of America found in a 2006 survey of 1,000 firms….**As for younger folks, the law permits them to get in-service distributions** of money rolled over from previous 401(k)s; of employer (but not employee) pretax contributions; of employee after-tax contributions; and of account earnings contributing to the plan…" (10)*

"There are many advantages of In-Service, Non-Hardship Distributions.

1. **Create Income Solutions.** As I mentioned in the previous chapter, you can create numerous plans for retirement income guaranteed using annuities that aren't available in most 401(k) plans. Remember when it comes to income, guarantees are extremely important. A "hope and a prayer" plan does not get it done. 401(k) plans offer little else by way of withdrawals.
2. **Diversity.** The options of the investment universe open up to you outside a 401(k) plan. This is especially true for the conservative investor seeking to put a portion of their retirement assets in protected vehicles. Remember the three Green Money Rules and they are available outside the 401(k) plan.
3. **Qualified Plan Consolidation.** If you are tired of getting statements from various IRA's, 401(k)'s, 403(b)'s or other plans representing the companies you worked with and want to consolidate them altogether under one roof it is available only outside your 401(k) plan. Isn't it true that as you get older you tend to forget more and long for simplicity.
4. **More Beneficiary Options.** Much like the lack of investment options for conservative investors, the 401(k) plan offers limited opportunities for serious estate planning.
5. **Availability of Stretch IRA.** No doubt about it, not using a Stretch IRA or Multi-Generational IRA format can cost your family millions. Don't miss this one.
6. **Get Some Professional Help if Desired.** There is also a universe of professionals available to you outside your 401(k) Plan. If you want to rid yourself of the disconnect between Wall Street and your retirement account, find a planner who understands the ABC's of Conservative Investing and get the protection you desire for the money you plan to live on the rest of your life."

Financial ABC's of retirement planning

Chapter Eleven Notes

FINANCIAL ABC's
of retirement planning

Chapter Twelve

You Need a Sherpa
How to Choose an Advisor

12.1   What are the qualities you look for in an advisor?

"How do you find a Sherpa, a financial planner that fits what you need? Many in the financial industry and academia will give you a laundry list of questions, qualities, and designations that will make you feel very insecure. I believe there are three important characteristics to consider when looking for a planner: trust, like-ability, and competence."

Trust

"Obviously one of the key characteristics, if not the most essential quality of a planner, is integrity. The planner must be someone you can trust not only with your most personal financial information, but detailed family matters that impact your finances. You must be able to trust their ability to remain confidential, not sharing your personal information with other clients or those outside their practice who might profit from your information."

"We know trust is something that is earned over time in a relationship. Unless you have missed something along the line, business is relational top to bottom. Trust in a relationship is earned when people do what they say they are going to do when they say they are going to do it. Trust is earned when planners anticipate the needs of a client and communicate on a regular basis. One of the sure keys to a trustworthy advisor is his method and amount of communication with his clients. Some use stale newsletters as the only way they communicate, or statements that seem to be written in Egyptian Hieroglyphics. How a planner communicates in a personal manner on an individual basis and what initiates that conversation is incredibly important."

12.2 What are your expectations for communication with your financial advisor?

"If trust is earned over time, how do you go about finding someone who can help get your initial ABC plan together? I suggest you "borrow" some trust. You probably have some friends who have a relationship with a planner. Ask them about their experience in working with their planner and if it sounds good to you, visit with the planner. You can "borrow" your friend's already developed trust, until you develop your own trust.

Another way to check on the credibility of an advisor is to ask the planner to let you call a couple of their current clients. Of course, they will give you only the clients they have a good relationship with, but that's fine. Call their clients and ask them to tell you about their "experience" of working with the planner. What is his style of communication? How do you feel when they are explaining investment options to you? Does he talk down to you or over your head? Do they communicate regularly?

Notice all these questions relate to the "experience" of working with a planner. We are trying to get a feel for how they trust their planner, not whether he's competent or not. You may want to ask them about the investments, but there are two things wrong with that question. First, you are now entering personal information territory. Most people don't want to reveal the types of assets and the performance of those assets, considering it is personal information. Second, most people don't understand the details and nuances of the investments they have. They could give you totally inaccurate information. This type of information you need to receive from the planner themselves.

Finally, you could attend a planner's workshop, if they conduct them, and get a feel for who they are as they relate with other people. Some planners may have great relationships with clients, but are somewhat uncomfortable up in front of a group, so this isn't the best way to determine the character of your potential planner. Yet, often a series of workshops conducted by a planner may give you the opportunity to check them out in a classroom style setting over a two- to three-session event."

12.3 In what ways would you check out the integrity of a financial advisor?

Like-ability

"The question is, is he or she the "kind of person" you would want to work with? You really don't want to dread the communication from your planner. I know I'm going to hurt someone's feelings here, but if calling your financial planner for assistance is anything like calling your dentist for a root canal, you have the wrong guy (sorry, dentists)."

12.4 **How important do you think it is to "like" the planner you are working with?**

"How do you determine what the "kind of person" is the planner you would like to work with? First, you have to know a little about yourself. In doing so, I think Tim Templeton's description of four business temperaments in his book *The Referral of a Lifetime* (3) might be helpful. I'll attempt to describe them, though the labels are Tim's:

Relational/Relational: These are folks who start and end with the love of relationships. They are people-people inside and out. Somehow business just happens.

Relational/Business: R/B people have an easy time developing relationships, but when the topic turns to business, they quickly get in to tactical mode.

Business/Relational: B/R people may be a little uncomfortable with relationships upfront and use "business talk" as a way to get started. However, once people become their clients, the relationships are long and fulfilling. They have very loyal clients.

Business/Business: B/B people are those who are not relationally motivated on the front end or the back end of a business relationship. They are business all the time and somehow relationships happen. It's wrong to think that this is not the kind of person you would want simply because of the business nature of the advisor. There are people who need financial advice that are B/B also, and the R/R person irritates them to no end! (4)"

12.5 **What type of business temperament do you think you are? Explain.**

"The key is to identify what type you are and then find the planner who fits your mold. Be aware that you will typically be a good fit with 3 out of the 4 temperaments."

Competence

"By competence, I mean they have acquired enough experience and knowledge to do the task you need done. You can investigate this again by asking for referrals and asking their clients about the advisor's competence. Visiting the advisor's workshops and client events are other ways of hearing them espouse their philosophy and financial planning techniques."

12.6 **How could the competence of an advisor affect the plan he would develop for you?**

12.7 **What are the steps you would take to determine an advisor's competence?**

"There are varying levels of financial planning in the industry. The Board of Certified Financial Planners considers three types of financial planning, all of which require different levels of information and training, yet all require the advisor to be diligent in his efforts and knowledgeable about the tasks.

The first is a single-issue plan. In other words, you need one facet of your finances dealt with in a competent manner, such as life insurance, or an annuity. You find a planner with an expertise in that asset and use them for your planning needs.

Second, you have a multi-strategy approach combining several types of assets in a financial plan. The plan may include Life Insurance, Health Insurance, and an annuity.

Lastly, you might need a comprehensive plan that involves everything you do financially. Life insurance, annuities, health insurance, property casualty insurance, tax planning, mutual funds, stocks, bonds, and even a revocable trust might be needed to accomplish your planning desires. For this, you would need an advisor who would quarterback a team of professionals.

The CFP Board considers all of these valid types of financial plans. Obviously, these three types of planning require varying degrees of competence. (5)"

"Find someone who, like the famous football Coach Vince Lombardi, is chasing perfection and catching a little excellence along the way."

Questions You Might Ask a Potential Advisor

"Questions You Might Ask a Potential Advisor:

- What is your area of specialty? Do you have an area of focus?
- What is your investment philosophy?
- How long have you been a planner?
- If you haven't been in the business long, who do you have as a mentor or back-up planner to help you plan?
- What licenses do you hold? Why those licenses?
- Do you have a planning team that includes attorneys or accountants or other advisors?
- Can I speak with 3-4 of your clients?
- Are you familiar with the ABC Model of Investing and do you use it in your planning?
- How do you make use of Fixed Index Annuities in your practice?
- Do you consider yourself a "safe money specialist?"
- Tell me about the manner in which you communicate with your clients.
    - Do you have client events?
    - Do you have a newsletter?
- Do you conduct regular reviews with your clients, and if so, how often?
- If I have a question after I become a client of yours, whom do I speak with?
- What types of assets do you use in planning?
- Can I visit your next client event?
- Are there any fees in working with you?
- Tell me about the planning process.
- Have you ever had any regulatory actions taken against you?

These are not an exhaustive list of questions, but it will definitely get you on the right road"

12.8 Highlight the questions you think are important. What other questions might you ask a potential advisor?

Becoming a Client-Partner

"First, I want to say that as a planner, I hate asking for referrals. It's uncomfortable for me and for my clients. I think its imposing on them. Advisors have used the same tired old tactics to ask for referrals forever. It is distasteful. I just don't believe in it.

Something I do believe in is a partnership between the client and advisor. The advisor's role is to create, implement, and adjust the financial plan tailored to the needs of the client. The advisor is partnering with the client to see them succeed in their retirement. Partnership is a two-way street by definition. The role of this client partnership is very important.

The role of the Client-Partner is to talk with others about the experience of working with the advisor and invite them to meet the advisor at a client event, workshop, or at an individual conference. As you are out in the community with your friends, family, and acquaintances, the subject of finances comes up. All you need to do is say, "you might want to speak with my advisor Dave." If they say they already have an advisor, drop the subject. Yet, if they ask you who your advisor is, tell them about the "experience" of working with him. Then simply invite them to meet with you and your advisor for lunch (the advisor will pay), or invite them to the next client event or workshop. This will enable your friend to meet your advisor in a casual setting to see if your advisor is the "kind of person" they might want to work with."

12.9 What has been your experience in referring an advisor?

12.10 How important to you is a client-partner relationship? Explain.

Chapter Twelve Notes

Chapter Thirteen

Deal or No Deal
Process, Process, Process

Three Elements of a Financial Decision

"It's a very interesting study when we look into the factors that affect our decision making. I believe there are three aspects of making decisions regarding financial planning: logic, emotion, and beliefs. (1)"

13.1 **What key elements are involved for you when making a financial decision?**

Logic

"First, is the area of logic—the science of reasoning. In other words, it's how we "make sense" of something. We have an innate need to reasonably work through an issue with facts and details. We need to rationally decide on an issue.

One of the problems Wall Street has is its inability to be rational. The Wall Street mentality, "greed is good" is a prime example. The Wall Street retirement philosophy has been advertised with life lived on a five-star golf course, vacations all over the world, hot cars, expensive jewelry, and a mystical green path directing you to your own personal pot of gold. Wall Street says you have a "number" and your "number" takes a beating in a nasty world, but they can magically protect your "number" with mutual fund pixie dust.

If you buy into the media fantasies of Wall Street greed, then you will spend your retirement chasing after money and making the materialistic goal of outgaining your neighbors your priority. In the end, much like Wall Street you are chasing the wind and you will always have a deeply seeded feeling of anxiety and frustration with your results. Who can catch the wind? You? Someone will always have more than you do, their funds will gain more than yours, and they will have more "stuff." You can spend an entire lifetime chasing the wind only to find out it can't be caught. Greed is not good."

13.2 Do you agree or disagree with the comments about Wall Street's "greed is good" philosophy? Explain.

"You need to see how a plan works "realistically" and not with a greedy goal. That's why ABC Investing is so important. You need to have real guarantees where they are needed, especially when it comes to income planning. Not a false promise of "safety" while being exposed to credit risk.

You need to be able to look at your plan and say to yourself, "Now, that makes sense!"

13.3 In what ways does your current plan make sense to you?

Beliefs

"Secondly, beliefs can be the stimulus for either a good or bad buying decision. What you believe about a topic will eventually determine how you feel about it. Counselors spend hours and hours trying to discover the beliefs of their patients driving their behaviors. For instance, if you have an underlying belief that money is evil, you will continually battle the idea of making more of it. If you believe money is king, then you won't be satisfied until you've tried every avenue leaving no stone unturned, including shady investment schemes, to try and get rich. Beliefs matter.

I have often told my son, "…emotions will eventually follow what you believe to be true, so *find out what the truth is and believe that*…your emotions will catch up eventually." Our emotions follow what we believe. We tend to get it backwards and follow our emotions far too much, so beliefs are crucial.

Wall Street tries its best to instill a belief system that is disconnected from reality at its best. If you believe that brokers are in the business only to make money at the expense of their clients, then you will have trouble listening to and following professional advice. If you believe only "irrational" people would buy an index annuity, then you will run the other way missing out on the guarantees. If you believe large wire houses are the only place to get professional advice, then you will miss out on some incredibly talented professionals, while buying into the greed is good mentality."

"A fictional belief is something we believe in that just isn't true. We acquired the belief through the media, friends, neighbors, brokers or other venues that we trust, yet the information is incorrect or the conclusions are skewed. We compile these beliefs over time and they dramatically affect the decisions we make."

13.4 Are you aware of any bias you hold regarding your assets? Explain.

13.5 How do you think your bias would affect your retirement planning?

"One of the realities that every investor has to deal with is "bias," which is a belief which prevents an unprejudiced consideration of a position. Bias is a distorted view that prevents impartiality. (2) Everyone has a bias. I have a bias. I am a conservative advisor whose career started in the insurance industry and added securities, or risk products, along the way. Authors who write articles for financial magazines, or analysts on financial television and radio shows, all have a background that lends itself to bias. No one is free of it."

13.6 Can you think of any examples of bias in the media regarding retirement planning?

"Your job is to "find out the truth and deal with that." What is truth? (Now there's an age-old question.) The truth deals with realism and facts. You have to be open to the reality that what you believe may in fact come from a bias, which can prevent you from making the most beneficial of plans. This is especially true in conservative investing. There are planners whose bias lends them to the belief every financial goal can be accomplished through the use of securities like stocks, bonds, mutual funds, derivatives, etc. This is simply not true."

"On the other hand, there are agents in the insurance industry that believe securities are too risky for retirees and index annuities are the only answer. They too are wrong. Even though a conservative investor may not want market risk, it doesn't mean all their money should be placed in annuities.

Challenge your beliefs. You have had a mental intravenous feeding of Wall Street's philosophy day in and day out. Challenge it. A conservative investor has to fly in the face of Wall Street beliefs. That's why the ABC Model helps a conservative investor determine how much risk to allow into their portfolio."

13.7 Do you have any beliefs about assets or groups of assets that need to be challenged? Explain.

Emotions

"…every study in academia shows buying is an emotional decision. Make no mistake about it. When you are planning your retirement and choosing conservative methods and financial tools, your emotions are fully engaged.

In fact, there are whole divisions within universities that study the emotional dynamics of investing labeled "behavioral finance," along with the impact of emotions on economies. John W. Rogers, Jr. emphasizes the point in his column "The Patient Investor" on Forbes.com:"

> "…behavioral academics are on the firmest ground citing the madness-of-crowds phenomenon. Most people make the same mistakes over and over. The most prevalent one is to pile in at the peak with everyone else. Since fitting in is easier than sticking out, investors flock together even when the results turn out bad." (3)

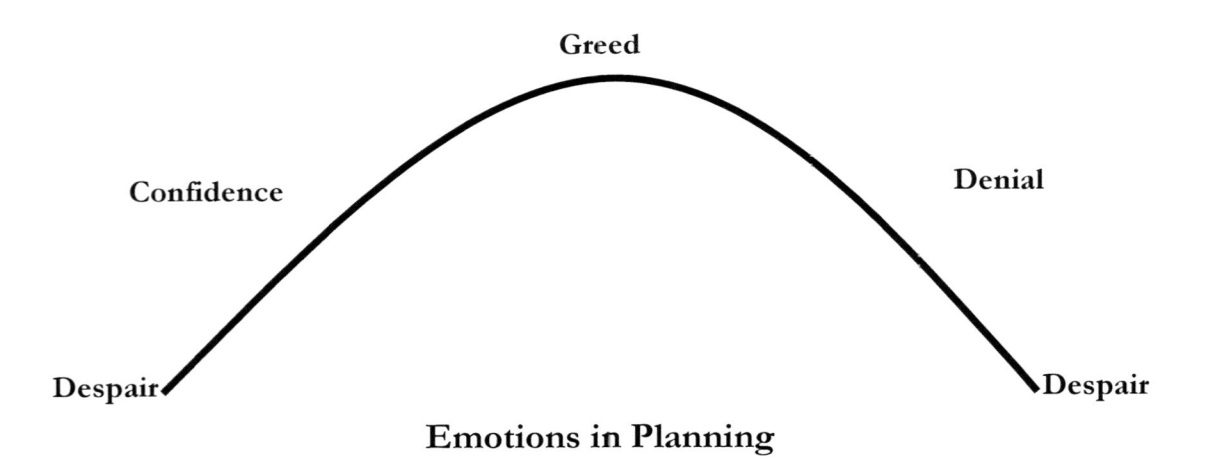

Emotions in Planning

(Graph: arc with labels — Despair (left), Confidence, Greed (top), Denial, Despair (right))

13.8 On the graph above, put an "X" on the line where you believe most people buy into the market, and an "O" on the line where you believe people typically sell out of the market. Explain your answer.

"In a typical Boom/Bust market cycle people are most often joining a "Buying Spree" near the top of the Bull market when enthusiasm is high. Then investors typically participate in a "Selling Spree" near the bottom of the market in a panic. This "madness-of-crowds phenomenon" runs in contrast to the age-old "buy low, sell high" axiom which instructs us to make the most out of the market by buying when it is at the bottom and selling out when you have made money. Remember, Baron Rothschild's advice on when to buy is when there is "blood in the streets." (4)

13.9 In the past, how have you let emotions affect your retirement planning decisions?

"As I have stated earlier, your emotions are valid when determining how much risk you want in your portfolio. Risk is how you "feel" about uncertainty in the market. Using a risk tolerance questionnaire can facilitate a more objective evaluation of how much risk you want in a portfolio. You don't need a questionnaire to find out if you are conservative. You already know that. What you need to work through emotions when investing is a sound planning process."

Process, Process, Process

"In battling emotional investing, you need a process to work through to protect yourself from making a potentially devastating purchasing decision. I suggest a process of investigation, recommendation, and implementation, followed by a healthy dose of review and adjustments. This process should help you work through your emotions, challenge your beliefs, and reasonably pursue a financial decision. The process should give you the time to make an informed decision.

Different planners plan differently. You can set your own pace in a decision making process by establishing the ground rules at the beginning of your work with an advisor. Knowing a simple planning system you can use with advisors will be helpful.

The first planning step is "investigation." During this step, you will discover all the risk, leaks, and gaps in your current financial plan. You should fill out a financial review form listing all your assets (appendix chapter one) and income. The financial review form can help you see your assets as a whole and how they relate to each other. You will want to list the concerns you have about your assets, your goals, and of course decide on the ABC Allocation you believe best fits you. You will want to pay close attention to the time horizon you have for your goals. This is crucial when it comes to deciding on the assets you use in your plan. An advisor can help you think through possible solutions to the concerns and goals you have.

Second, either develop for yourself or receive from an advisor a plan which includes everything your goals set out to accomplish. This plan should be detailed and involve assets and income from specific sources. The plan should include what you want to accomplish in at least the next five years with an ability to adjust as necessary.

Third, implement your plan when you have worked out the details and you are confident it is a solution to problems—one that will accomplish your goals. It will involve a lot of paperwork and is best done in a separate meeting so you have time to go over the details with your advisor. You will most likely have to make transfers into different companies, which will create a conservation attempt in some form, by the current company holding your money. Just remember, it's your money, not theirs. This is something they often forget.

Lastly, you will want to review the plan once all the monies are transferred to make sure they are where you wanted them to be and in the amounts you had determined for your plan. I would suggest you review the plan at least every six months to make sure you are on the right path. If you have assets in Column C, the Red Risk portion, you will want some type of a review quarterly. Remember your goals and especially your time horizon. For conservative investors this is not a sprint, but a marathon."

"Given the right process, your emotions will be given the opportunity to be led by your beliefs, which will be challenged by the truth, leading to a logical conclusion."

13.10 How important to you is using a good financial decision making process? Explain.

Chapter Thirteen Notes

FINANCIAL ABC's
of retirement planning

Chapter Fourteen

Seven Steps to an ABC Plan

Step One: Get Your Assets Together

"Begin by gathering your most recent asset statements. The following is a partial list of statements to gather:
- Brokerage accounts
- Mutual funds
- IRA, 401(k), 403(b) and other qualified plans
- Annuities
- Bank accounts, including CD's, savings, and money market accounts
- Stock certificates
- Bonds, including government savings bonds
- Life Insurance
- Precious Metals
- Real Estate

Take the statements to your advisor and they will gladly make you copies. Use one of the Asset Review Forms in Appendix One to assist you in arranging your finances so you can see the "big picture." Getting all your assets together and making a list benefits you in many ways. If something were to happen to you, your spouse or heirs would have a current list of assets. It also helps your think more clearly about your finances rather than having a scattered idea of what you own."

Step Two: Write It Down

"Using the forms in Appendixes One and Two to write down your thoughts will help organize your thinking before seeing an advisor. You will want to write down the greatest concerns you have about your assets and your goals for the near and far future.

Write down some of the things that worry you most about your financial situation. If you can't think of any big worries, then remember everyone has a "pebble in the shoe." In other words, something which may be small, but it irritates the heck out you. If you have ever had a pebble in your shoe when walking or running a long distance and ended up with a huge blister or sore on your foot, you know exactly what I'm talking about. If you have a pebble in the shoe financially, now is the time to deal with it. It may be a certain asset like a bond, or mutual fund you've had a long time and isn't a lot of money, but it has frustrated you the whole time you have had it.

Your frustrations and fears can also be large enough to keep you awake at night. Maybe you are struggling to gain enough assets to retire on, or your income is changing soon and you're not sure how to replace it. Your current advisor might not communicate with you, or you are just worried about the path the economy is on and want off the roller coaster. All of these are valid and need to be expressed on the list.

Written goals are a sure way to guarantee you will be able to know if you are on track with your investments. You will want to write down immediate goals, 1 year, 3 year, 5 year and even longer goals. You can always adjust your goals, but if you don't have anything to adjust, you end up lost. Remember, if you don't have a target to shoot at, you'll end up hitting anything."

Step Three: ABC Your Assets

"Now you are ready to choose which types of assets you would want to invest in going forward. Pretend every asset is moveable and changeable, and then ask yourself if you could make a new plan starting today, what would that plan look like? You will want to distinguish your investible assets from your non-liquid assets. For instance, you might have invested in a rental home, which isn't a liquid asset, as opposed to a stock or mutual fund. Be sure and get a total of "investible assets" before trying to ABC them.

Remember there are three categories of assets Yellow, Green, and Red. What percent of your assets do you need in cash for emergencies, coming events, and if your income dries up for six months to a year? This is Yellow Column A money. Next, what percent do you want in the market with either bond-type risk or stock-type risk? This is Red Column C money. Finally, add the two percentages you just wrote down and subtract it from 100, and this is the amount of money you want in the Green Column B. Keep in mind, the three Green Money rules which reduce market risk in your portfolio. Make use of the last page of the Financial Review Form in Appendix One."

Step Four: Choose an Advisor

"Deciding to take this step of finding an advisor means you are serious about your planning needs and want a conservative advisor. Go back to chapter 13 and figure out which temperament you are, then begin asking your friends about their advisors or visit a few seminars and workshops."

"Next, look over the questions to ask an advisor in Chapter 12 and take them with you to interview your prospective agent. You might very well be in a class going over this material and the advisor you've spent time with seems to your liking. Run through the questions with them. Once you are satisfied that they understand conservative investing and they have demonstrated a competence, go ahead to Step Five.

Just a thought. Whether your advisor is an insurance agent or a securities broker, or both, doesn't matter. You want someone who understands the ABC's of Conservative Investing and is able to facilitate that style of plan for your benefit. There are many, many different types of financial licenses and designations, but in the long run, they need to understand you, how you want to invest conservatively, and do it competently."

Step Five: Process, Process, Process

"Now is the time to work through a planning process with the advisor. If he is trained in the ABC's, then he or she is familiar with the steps of Investigate, Recommend, Implement, Review and Adjust. These steps will help you challenge your fictional beliefs, and work through your emotions while travelling down a logical path to financial success.

I find the plan will come with two facets: overview and detail. You will want to understand the "big picture" of your plan while also digging into details."

Step Six: Review & Adjust

"Once you have implemented your plan with the advisor, decide on a schedule of reviews that meets your needs best. Get on their calendar right away, as it will give you confidence knowing you have the opportunity to review the plan again and see if it is going according to the projections and parameters you originally laid out.

It's also in this step that you take the initiative of a "client-partner." If you have had a good experience with your advisor, then "talk him up" to your family and friends. Ask your advisor for his calendar of client events so you can become part of the group and bring your friends who have expressed an interest in the advisor's services."

Step Seven: Sleep Easy

"You can actually enjoy a good night's rest knowing that your ABC Plan has just the right amount of risk in it that only you can handle. It's your plan, not a Wall Street broker's plan.

In the end, conservative investing isn't anything like Batman socks or other fads. It is not the flavor of the month style of investing that has caught so many investors by surprise in a down market. Conservative investing is long-haul, core investing with just the right amount of risk tailored to your temperament.

My hope is that you have indeed resonated with the concepts involved in the ABC's of Conservative Investing and are willing to begin your seven steps to a peaceful night's rest."

14.1 **In what ways have you "resonated" with the Financial ABC's of Retirement Planning?**

14.2 **How will you use the ABC Planning Model in your current situation? Will you seek out an advisor familiar with the ABC Model?**

Chapter Fourteen Notes

Financial ABC's of retirement planning

Appendixes

FINANCIAL ABC's
of retirement planning

Appendix One

ASSET REVIEW FORMS

On the following pages are two forms, the "Issues and Goals Review Form" and the "Financial Planning Data Form." The Issues and Goals form can be used to sort out your feelings surrounding the issues in financial planning and the goals you want to accomplish. These forms will help you accomplish steps two and three of "The ABC Plan in Seven Steps" outlined in Chapter 14.

The Financial Planning Data Form on the following pages will assist you in logging information needed to create your financial plan. It will also assist your ABC Financial Planner in understanding how you view of your assets.

Just take your time as you answer the questions; discuss them with your spouse, significant other, close friend, or financial advisor if possible. One of the best things you could do is to fill it out two different times, sharpening your thoughts each time

FINANCIAL ABC's
of retirement planning

Issues & Goals Review Form
What's Important to You?
(These are questions to help you discover your highest value needs.)

What is it that you were hoping to accomplish by making a financial plan?

What is important to you about?

1. Taxes

2. Safety

3. Guarantees

4. Long Term Care Planning

5. Achieving Security

Issues & Goals Review Form
What's Important to You?
Cont'd

6. Income

7. Liquidity

8. Return on Assets

9. Diversification

10. Inflation

11. Passing Assets on to Heirs

12. Communication with your Agent/Broker

FINANCIAL ABC's
of retirement planning

Highest Relational Needs & Expectations
What's Important to You?
(These are questions to help you discover your "rules for change".)

1. Of all the concerns listed above, how would you prioritize the importance of what you want to work on?

    a. What do you like or dislike about your current financial plan?

    b. How would you define success in your financial plan?

    c. What would you change?

    d. How do you determine "next steps"?

    e. What is your past experience with planners?

    f. What will be the response of your current advisor if you make changes with a different advisor?

    g. How would you respond?

    h. Who do you include when making decisions of this nature?

2. If you haven't solved these issues to date, why is it important that you take action now?

3. What are the most important things to you when it comes to partnering with a professional advisor?

4. If you could wave a magic wand and solve these issues, what would it look like?

FINANCIAL ABC's
of retirement planning

Short & Long Term Goals

(These questions will help you think through your immediate, short-term, and long-term goals.)

1. Do you live off the interest income of your assets?
    a. What is the amount of income derived from your assets?

2. Are you satisfied with your current income?
    a. If "No", explain.

3. Do you anticipate any changes in your annual income?
    a. If "Yes", explain.

4. Are you planning any major lifestyle changes?
    a. If "Yes", explain.

5. Do you see any large purchases in the next 2 to 5 years?
    a. If "Yes", explain.

FINANCIAL ABC's
of retirement planning

Short & Long Term Goals – Cont'd

Rate the importance of the items below from 1 (most important) to 5 (least important).

    b. Pay less income tax:___

    c. Reduce or eliminate estate tax:___

    d. Reduce or eliminate capital gains tax:___

    e. Increase monthly income:___

    f. Finding a good money manager for assets in the market:___

    g. Ensure that my assets are protected from market losses:___

    h. Increase my returns on savings and retirement funds:___

    i. Protection of principal:___

6. What do you want to accomplish with your assets over the next two years?

7. List three financial goals for the next three to five years?

8. List two financial goals for ten years from now?

9. List two financial goals beyond ten years?

FINANCIAL ABC's
of retirement planning

Financial Planning Data Form
Family Information

Person #1: _____ Age:_____ **M**   **D**   **W**   **NM**
(Key: **M**arried/**D**ivorced/**W**idowed/**N**ot **M**arried)
SS#: ____-___-____ DOB: ___/___/___ Citizen of U.S. __Yes __No

Person #2: _____ Age:_____ **M**   **D**   **W**   **NM**
(Key: **M**arried/**D**ivorced/**W**idowed/**N**ot **M**arried)
SS#: ____-___-____ DOB: ___/___/___ Citizen of U.S. __Yes __No

Address: _____ County: _____

City: _____ State: _____ Zip: _____

Home Phone: _____-_____-_____ Work Phone: _____-_____-_____

Children:___

Name:_____ Age:_____   **M**   **D**   **W**   **NM**
City/St:_____

Name:_____ Age:_____   **M**   **D**   **W**   **NM**
City/St:_____

Name:_____ Age:_____   **M**   **D**   **W**   **NM**
City/St:_____

Name:_____ Age:_____   **M**   **D**   **W**   **NM**
City/St:_____

Name:_____ Age:_____   **M**   **D**   **W**   **NM**
City/St:_____

Name:_____ Age:_____   **M**   **D**   **W**   **NM**
City/St:_____

Retirement Date(s):
Person #1:_____ Person #2:_____
Do you have a will? **Yes**   **No**   Do you have a trust? **Yes**   **No**
Type of trust:_____

Do you have a Property & Financial POA? **Yes**   **No**
Do you have a Health Care POA? **Yes**   **No**   Living Will? **Yes**   **No**
Disability: **Yes**   **No**
Notes:

FINANCIAL ABC's
of retirement planning

Financial Information

ASSETS	Cost Basis	Present Value	
Real Estate			Mortgage? Equity Loan?
Home	_____	_____	_____
Other Real Estate	_____	_____	_____
	_____	_____	_____
	_____	_____	_____

Cash
Stocks
Bonds
Mutual Funds
Business Interests
Other Assets
CDs & Savings Accts.
Checking Accts.

Personal Property
Home Furnishings,
Jewelry, Silverware,
Antiques, & Collectibles

Sub-Total - A _____

Primary Financial Objective
(Rank in order of importance):
____ Tax Deferral
____ Income Now
____ Growth
____ Estate Planning
____ Preservation of Principal
____ Other _____

Willingness to Accept Risk for Additional Financial Performance (Choose One):
____ Aggressive
____ Moderate
____ Conservative

IRA's & Insurance
Husband's IRA
Wife's IRA
Pension (401, etc.)
Life Insurance
Face Value/Cash Value
_____/_____
_____/_____
_____/_____

Annuities   Fixed   FIA   VA
_____   ___   ___   ___
_____   ___   ___   ___
_____   ___   ___   ___

Sub-Total - B _____
TOTAL – A+B _____

Income
_____ Husband's SS
_____ Wife's SS
_____ Pension
_____ Pension
_____ W2/1099
_____ W2/1099
_____ Other
_____ **Total**

Estimated Federal Tax Bracket:
____ 0-15%
____ 16-28%
____ 29-35%
____ 36% & up

ABC Profile

A	B	C	Comments
Cash Potentially Lower Returns Liquid & Taxable	**Protected Growth** Potentially Moderate Returns Offers Partial Withdrawals & Tax Deferral	**Risk Growth** Potentially Higher Returns Liquid & Taxable Stock Type Risk Bond Type Risk	
Preferred Percent in This Category	Preferred Percent in This Category	Preferred Percent in This Category	
Estimated Percent Already in This Category	Estimated Percent Already in This Category	Estimated Percent Already in This Category	

FINANCIAL ABC's
of retirement planning

Appendix Two

RETIREMENT BUDGET WORKSHEET

On the following pages you will find a sample retirement budget worksheet. Fill this form out when you are planning to retire in order to determine how much income you'll need in retirement. The form can also be used before retirement to anticipate the effects of major lifestyle changes such as a change in occupation or the death of a spouse.

Simply fill in the first column according to your current income and expenses. The second column is what you anticipate to spend. Subtract the second column from the first column and you will be able to determine what you will need for income when you retire.

Retirement Budget Worksheet

Expenses			
Item	Current Budget	Retirement Budget	Difference
Residence			
Rent or mortgage			
Real estate taxes			
Home Owners/Renters Insurance			
Furniture and furnishings			
Appliances			
Cleaning, repairs and maintenance			
Electricity, gas and heating			
Water and sewer			
Telephone, cell phone, cable			
Other			
Total Residence			
Meals & Groceries			
Groceries & meals at home			
Meals outside the home			
Total Meals & Groceries			
Clothing			
Clothing, shoes, jackets, etc.			
Dry cleaning, laundry			
Jewelry			
Total Clothing			

Personal			
Personal care and toiletries			
Child care			
Legal and accounting			
Life and disability insurance			
Other			
Total personal			
Transportation			
Vehicle payments			
Repairs and maintenance			
Insurance			
Gas, oil and tires			
Public transportation			
Other			
Total Transportation			
Healthcare			
Prescriptions			
Doctors, dentists and hospitals			
Health insurance			
Other			
Total Healthcare			
Debt, Savings and Investments			
Credit cards & other loans			
Investment dollars			
Emergency fund			
Vacation & entertainment savings			
Debt removal			
Other			
Total Debt, Savings & Investments			
Miscellaneous			
Books & other publications			
Vacations			
Entertainment and affiliations			
Charitable giving			
Education			
Investment costs			
Other			
Total Miscellaneous			
Total Expenses			
Income			
Item	**Current Budget**	**Retirement Budget**	**Difference**
Salary & Wages			
1099 Income			
Rental Income			
Dividends			
Interest			
Sale of assets			

Social Security			
Pensions			
Other			
Total Income			
Net Income & Expenses			

Financial ABC's of retirement planning

Appendix Three

Risk Tolerance Questionnaire

Please place the score on the line to the right by writing the number on the line.

1. **What is the time horizon (prior to income or systematic withdrawals) for this investment account?**
   (EXAMPLE: answer a. would be a score of 0 on the line.)
   - a. Less than 3 years   _____ a. 0
   - b. 3 to 5 years   _____ b. 5
   - c. 5 to 10 years   _____ c. 7
   - d. 10 to 15 years   _____ d. 10
   - e. Greater than 15 years   _____ e. 15

2. **What percentage of your liquid net worth is in principal protected products (i.e., Fixed Annuities, CDs, Life Insurance)?**
   - a. Less than 10%   _____ a. 3
   - b. Between 10% and 25%   _____ b. 5
   - c. Between 25% and 50%   _____ c. 7
   - d. Between 50% and 75%   _____ d. 10
   - e. Greater than 75%   _____ d. 15

3. **Investments that provide greater returns over the long run often are more volatile over the short run. Choose the answer that best describes your concerns about value changes:**
   a) Day-to-day fluctuations in the value of my investments make me very uncomfortable.
   - a. Strongly Agree   _____ a. 1
   - b. Agree   _____ b. 2
   - c. Neutral   _____ c. 3
   - d. Disagree   _____ d. 4
   - e. Strongly Disagree   _____ e. 5

   b) Short-term volatility is acceptable when prospects of greater long-term gains exist.
   - a. Strongly Agree   _____ a. 5
   - b. Agree   _____ b. 4
   - c. Neutral   _____ c. 3
   - d. Disagree   _____ d. 2
   - e. Strongly Disagree   _____ e. 1

4. In the first year, if these assets lose 1/3 of their total value, but evidence suggests that the portfolio should probably recover enough to still meet your goal, how would you react?

   a) Short-term losses are unacceptable even if historical evidence suggests my long-term goal is still achievable

   a. Strongly Agree   ____a. 1
   b. Agree   ____b. 2
   c. Neutral   ____c. 3
   d. Disagree   ____d. 4
   e. Strongly Disagree   ____e. 5

   b) Short-term losses don't bother me as long as my long-term investment goal is still attainable.

   a. Strongly Agree   ____a. 5
   b. Agree   ____b. 4
   c. Neutral   ____c. 3
   d. Disagree   ____d. 2
   e. Strongly Disagree   ____e. 1

5. Expected Return. Determine which risk best fits you?
   Expected Average Return and Volatility (75% Probability) Expected Return:

   a. Volatility between -3% to 15%, expected return of 6%   ____a. 1
   b. Volatility between -4% to 18%, expected return of 7%   ____b. 3
   c. Volatility between -6% to 22%, expected return of 8%   ____c. 5
   d. Volatility between -10% to 30%, expected return of 10%   ____d. 7
   e. Volatility between -14% to 36%, expected return of 12%   ____e. 10

6. Choose the statement that best reflects your thoughts about reaching your financial goals: I am interested in stable growth in the value of my portfolio, even if it means accepting lower results in the long run.

   a. Strongly Agree   ____a. 1
   b. Agree   ____b. 3
   c. Neutral   ____c. 5
   d. Disagree   ____d. 7
   e. Strongly Disagree   ____e. 10

7. This investment represents approximately what percentage of your total investments, excluding your principal residence or vacation homes?

   a. Greater than 75%   ____a. 1
   b. Between 51% and 75%   ____b. 2
   c. Between 25% and 50%   ____c. 3
   d. Between 10% and 25%   ____d. 4
   e. Less than 10%   ____e. 5

**Your total score will help us determine the appropriate investment profile (below): _____
Total Score**

Total Score	Risk Profile
0 – 31	Conservative
32 – 63	Moderate
64 – 75	Aggressive

*Used by permission of Dan Hunt and Redhawk Wealth Advisors, Inc. 9/2010

Appendix Three

Endnotes

Chapter One
1. "What does risk mean?" Investopedia.com. 8 June 2010. <http://www.investopedia.com/terms/r/risk.asp>..
2. United States. Board of Governors Federal Reserve System. Instrument, "CDs (secondary market)", Maturity, "6-month". 6 June 2010 <http://www.federalreserve.gov/releases/h15/data/Annual/H15_CD_M6.txt>.

Chapter Two
1. YahooFinance.com. 11 August 2010. Dow Interactive Chart from 2000-2009. 11 August 2010. <http://finance.yahoo.com>.
2. "Invest". Merriam-Webster.com. 12 August 2010.. Merriam-Webster Online Dictionary, 2009. 12 August 2010 <http://www.merriam-webster.com/dictionary/invest>.
3. "Gamble". Merriam-Webster.com. 12 August 2010.. Merriam-Webster Online Dictionary, 2009. 12 August 2010 <http://www.merriam-webster.com/dictionary/gamble>.
4. Edward Winslow. Blind Faith. San Francisco: Berrett-Koehler Publishers, Inc., 2003
5. Edward Winslow. Blind Faith. San Francisco: Berrett-Koehler Publishers, Inc., 2003
6. "History of 401(k) Plans", Employee Benefit Research Institute, February 2005.
7. Investment Company Institute. The US Retirement Market 2007. Research Fundamentals. Vol. 17, No. 3. 2008.
8. "Dow Jones Industrial Average History". Dow Jones Indexes. <http://www.djindexes.com/djia2008/docs/djia-historical-components.pdf>. September 4, 2010
9. Russell Napier. The Anatomy of a Bear. Great Britain: Harriman House, Ltd., 2009
10. Russell Napier. The Anatomy of a Bear. Great Britain: Harriman House, Ltd., 2009

Chapter Three
1. "Funny Stockbroker Jokes" Workjoke.com. August 7, 2010. <http://www.workjoke.com/stockbrokers-jokes.html#739>.
2. "Wire House Broker" Investopedia.com. April 2009. <http://www.investopedia.com/terms/w/wire-house-broker.asp>.
3. "Warren Buffet Quotes" brainyquote.com, September 14, 2010.<http://www.brainyquote.com/quotes/authors/w/warren_buffett_3.html>.

4. Weininger, Bruce, CPA, CFP. "Euthanize Wealth Management Practices" <u>Investment Advisor Magazine</u>. July 2009: 68
5. Stein, Ben. "Lessons from a Very Bad Year." YahooFinance.com/<u>Personal Finance</u>. 22 Dec. 2008. <http://finance.yahoo.com/expert/article/yourlife/130751>.
6. <u>YahooFinance.com</u>. 22 Aug. 2010. S&P 500 Interactive Chart from 200-2009. <http://finance.yahoo.com>.
7. Cochrane, Tom. "An Interview with Wharton Professor David Babbel – Part One." <u>AnnuityDigest.com</u>, 26 July 2009. <http://www.annuitydigest.com/blog/tom/interview-wharton-professor-david-babbel-part-one>.
8. Babbel, David F. "<u>Un-supermodels and the FIA.</u>" Ibbotson Associates/IFID Centre Conference, University of Chicago – Gleacher Center. Guaranteed Living Income Benefit Insurance Products. November 11, 2008

Chapter Four
1. Samuelson, William, Boston University and Zeckhauser, Richard, Harvard University. "Status Quo Bias in Decision Making." Journal of Risk and Uncertainty. 1:7-59 (1988) Kluwer Academic Publishers, Boston
2. Elzweig, Mark. "Slash and Burn: The New Wall Street Growth Model" 8 Nov. 2009. <u>Investment News.com.</u> <http://www.investmentnews.com/apps/pbcs.dll/article?AID=/20091108/REG/311089985>.

Chapter Five
1. United States. Board of Governors Federal Reserve System. <u>Instrument, "CDs (secondary market)", Maturity, "6-month"</u>. 6 June 2010 <http://www.federalreserve.gov/releases/h15/data/Annual/H15_CD_M6.txt>.
2. "Current Annual Inflation Rate." <u>Inflationdata.com</u>. 16 Sept. 2010. Capital Professional Services, LLC. <<u>http://inflationdata.com/Inflation/Inflation_Rate/CurrentInflation.asp</u>>.
3. "Annuities Double CD Performance." <u>InsuranceNewsnet Magazine</u>. December 2008: 24.
4. <u>YahooFinance.com</u>. 14 Sept. 2010. S&P 500 Interactive Chart from 1995-1999. <http://finance.yahoo.com>.

Chapter Six
1. United States. Board of Governors Federal Reserve System. <u>Instrument, "CDs (secondary market)", Maturity, "6-month"</u>. 6 June 2010

Chapter Seven
1. "Dennis Green Meltdown." <u>YouTube.com.</u> 26 Oct. 2006. <http://www.youtube.com/watch?v=m_N1OjGhIFc>.

Chapter Eight
1. "Systematic Risk." <u>Investopedia.com.</u> 16 Sept. 2010. <http://www.investopedia.com/terms/s/systematicrisk.asp>.
2. "Standard Deviation" <u>Investopedia.com</u>. 16 Sept. 2010. <http://www.investopedia.com/terms/s/standarddeviation.asp>.
3. "R-Squared." <u>Investopedia.com</u>. 16 Sept. 2010. <<u>http://www.investopedia.com/terms/r/r-squared.asp</u>>.

4. YahooFinance.com. 22 Aug. 2010. CGM Focus Fund Performance. <http://finance.yahoo.com/q/pm?s=CGMFX+Performance>.
5. YahooFinance.com. 22 Aug. 2010. AGTHX Performance. <http://finance.yahoo.com/q/pm?s=AGTHX+Performance>.

Chapter Nine
1. "Bear Market." Investopedia.com. 16 Sept. 2010. <http://www.investopedia.com/terms/b/bearmarket.asp>.
2. Russell Napier. The Anatomy of a Bear. Great Britain: Harriman House, Ltd., 2009
3. "John D. Rockefeller Quotes." thinkexist.com. 22 Aug. 2010. John D. Rockefeller American Industrialist and philanthropist, founder of the Standard Oil Company, 1839-1937. <http://thinkexist.com/quotes/john_d._rockefeller/2.html>.
4. "Warren Buffett Quotes." BrainyQuote.com. 17 Sept. 2010. <http://www.brainyquote.com/quotes/authors/w/warren_buffett_2.html>.
5. Russell Napier. The Anatomy of a Bear. Great Britain: Harriman House, Ltd., 2009
6. YahooFinance.com. 22 Aug. 2010. S&P 500 Interactive Chart from 1995-1999. <http://finance.yahoo.com>.
7. Ibid.
8. "Warren Buffett Quotes." BrainyQuote.com, 17 Sept. 2010. <http://www.brainyquote.com/quotes/authors/w/warren_buffett_2.html>.

Chapter Ten
1. "What is the Average Retirement Age?" WiseGeek.com. 20 Sept. 2010. <http://www.wisegeek.com/what-is-the-average-retirement-age.htm>.
2. United States. Social Security Online. Period Life Table –Actuarial Publications. <http://www.ssa.gov/OACT/STATS/table4c6.html>.
3. YahooFinance.com. 20 Sept. 2010. S&P 500 Interactive Chart from 1995-1999. <http://finance.yahoo.com>.

Chapter Eleven
1. "History of 401(k) Plans: An Update, Facts from EBRI." EBRI.org. Feb. 2009. Employee Benefit Research Institute. 17 Aug. 2010. <http://www.ebri.org/pdf/publications/facts/0205fact.a.pdf>.
2. "The U.S. Retirement Market, 2007." ICI.org. Investment Company Institute. Research Fundamentals. July 2008. Vol. 17 No. 3A. < http://www.ici.org/pdf/fm-v17n3_appendix.pdf>.
3. United States. Internal Revenue Service. Department of the Treasury. EP Compliance Risk Assessments – 401(k) Plans. March 4, 2009. <http://www.irs.gov/retirement/article/0,,id=147172,00.html>.
4. Ibid.
5. Choate,Natalie. "Life and Deat Planning for Retirement Benefits: Sixth Edition, completely revised." Boston. Ataxplan Publications:2006.
6. Ibid.
7. Ibid.
8. Ibid.
9. Ibid.
10. Ebeling, Ashlea. "The Great 401(k) Escape." Forbes.com. 31 Jan. 2008. <http://www.forbes.com/forbes/2008/0225/046.html>.

Chapter Twelve
1. "Sir Edmund Hillary Biography: Conqueror of Mt. Everest." Achievement.org. Academy of Achievement. 10 Jan. 2008. <http://www.achievement.org/autodoc/page/hil0pro-1>.
2. Clark, Leisl and Salkeld, Audrey. "The Mystery of Mallory and Irvine '24" PBS.org. Nov. 2000. NOVA Online Adventure. 19 Aug. 2010. <http://www.pbs.org/wgbh/nova/everest/lost/mystery/>.
3. Templeton, Tim. The Referral of a Lifetime. San Francisco. Berrett-Koehler Publishers. 2003-2004
4. Ibid.
5. Taylor, Don A. and Worsham, C. Bruce. Financial Planning: Process and Environment. Bryn Mawr: The American College. 2007

Chapter Thirteen
1. Marion, Jack. Change Buyer Behavior and Sell More Annuities. Indexannuity.org. 2009 <http://www.indexannuity.org/Change%20Buyer%20Behavior%20(excerpts).pdf>
2. "Bias." Dictionary.com, 22 Sept. 2010. <http://dictionary.reference.com/browse/bias>.
3. Rogers, John W., Jr. "Emotional Investing." Forbes.com. The Patient Investor. 31 Oct. 2005. <http://www.forbes.com/forbes/2005/1031/218.html>.
4. Myers, Daniel, CFA. Buy When There's Blood in the Streets. Investopedia.com. 22 Sept. 2010. <http://www.investopedia.com/articles/financial-theory/08/contrarian-investing.asp>.

Chapter Fourteen
No Footnotes